CYBERBULLYING AND OTHER ONLINE SAFETY ISSUES FOR CHILDREN

United States Congress House of Representatives Committee on the Judiciary, Subcommittee on Crime, Terrorism, and Homeland Security

CYBERBULLYING AND OTHER ONLINE SAFETY ISSUES FOR CHILDREN

HEARING

BEFORE THE

SUBCOMMITTEE ON CRIME, TERRORISM, AND HOMELAND SECURITY

OF THE

COMMITTEE ON THE JUDICIARY
HOUSE OF REPRESENTATIVES

ONE HUNDRED ELEVENTH CONGRESS

FIRST SESSION

ON

H.R. 1966 and H.R. 3630

SEPTEMBER 30, 2009

Serial No. 111–76

Printed for the use of the Committee on the Judiciary

Available via the World Wide Web: http://judiciary.house.gov

U.S. GOVERNMENT PRINTING OFFICE

52–547 PDF WASHINGTON : 2010

For sale by the Superintendent of Documents, U.S. Government Printing Office
Internet: bookstore.gpo.gov Phone: toll free (866) 512–1800; DC area (202) 512–1800
Fax: (202) 512–2104 Mail: Stop IDCC, Washington, DC 20402–0001

COMMITTEE ON THE JUDICIARY

JOHN CONYERS, Jr., Michigan, *Chairman*

HOWARD L. BERMAN, California
RICK BOUCHER, Virginia
JERROLD NADLER, New York
ROBERT C. "BOBBY" SCOTT, Virginia
MELVIN L. WATT, North Carolina
ZOE LOFGREN, California
SHEILA JACKSON LEE, Texas
MAXINE WATERS, California
WILLIAM D. DELAHUNT, Massachusetts
ROBERT WEXLER, Florida
STEVE COHEN, Tennessee
HENRY C. "HANK" JOHNSON, Jr., Georgia
PEDRO PIERLUISI, Puerto Rico
MIKE QUIGLEY, Illinois
LUIS V. GUTIERREZ, Illinois
BRAD SHERMAN, California
TAMMY BALDWIN, Wisconsin
CHARLES A. GONZALEZ, Texas
ANTHONY D. WEINER, New York
ADAM B. SCHIFF, California
LINDA T. SÁNCHEZ, California
DEBBIE WASSERMAN SCHULTZ, Florida
DANIEL MAFFEI, New York

LAMAR SMITH, Texas
F. JAMES SENSENBRENNER, Jr., Wisconsin
HOWARD COBLE, North Carolina
ELTON GALLEGLY, California
BOB GOODLATTE, Virginia
DANIEL E. LUNGREN, California
DARRELL E. ISSA, California
J. RANDY FORBES, Virginia
STEVE KING, Iowa
TRENT FRANKS, Arizona
LOUIE GOHMERT, Texas
JIM JORDAN, Ohio
TED POE, Texas
JASON CHAFFETZ, Utah
TOM ROONEY, Florida
GREGG HARPER, Mississippi

PERRY APELBAUM, *Staff Director and Chief Counsel*
SEAN MCLAUGHLIN, *Minority Chief of Staff and General Counsel*

SUBCOMMITTEE ON CRIME, TERRORISM, AND HOMELAND SECURITY

ROBERT C. "BOBBY" SCOTT, Virginia, *Chairman*

PEDRO PIERLUISI, Puerto Rico
JERROLD NADLER, New York
ZOE LOFGREN, California
SHEILA JACKSON LEE, Texas
MAXINE WATERS, California
STEVE COHEN, Tennessee
ANTHONY D. WEINER, New York
DEBBIE WASSERMAN SCHULTZ, Florida
MIKE QUIGLEY, Illinois

LOUIE GOHMERT, Texas
TED POE, Texas
BOB GOODLATTE, Virginia
DANIEL E. LUNGREN, California
J. RANDY FORBES, Virginia
TOM ROONEY, Florida

BOBBY VASSAR, *Chief Counsel*
CAROLINE LYNCH, *Minority Counsel*

CONTENTS

SEPTEMBER 30, 2009

CYBERBULLYING AND OTHER ONLINE SAFETY ISSUES FOR CHILDREN

WEDNESDAY, SEPTEMBER 30, 2009

HOUSE OF REPRESENTATIVES,
SUBCOMMITTEE ON CRIME, TERRORISM,
AND HOMELAND SECURITY
COMMITTEE ON THE JUDICIARY,
Washington, DC.

The Subcommittee met, pursuant to notice, at 3:34 p.m., in room 2141, Rayburn House Office Building, the Honorable Robert C. "Bobby" Scott (Chairman of the Subcommittee) presiding.

Present: Representatives Scott, Wasserman Schultz, Gohmert, and Lungren.

Staff Present: (Majority) Bobby Vassar, Subcommittee Chief Counsel; Karen Wilkinson, Federal Public Defender Office Detailee; Joe Graupensperger, Counsel; Veronica Eligan, Professional Staff Member; and (Minority) Caroline Lynch, Counsel.

Mr. SCOTT. The Subcommittee will now come to order.

I am pleased to welcome you today to the hearing before the Subcommittee on Crime, Terrorism, and Homeland Security on "Cyberbullying and Other Online Safety Issues for Children."

The term "cyberbullying" has many different definitions and can cover many different types of speech. It can consist of rumors or lies, a publication of something meant to be private, or the impersonation of another person. Or it can encompass more problematic speech, involving threats, stalking, or predatory behavior.

The cyberbully can reveal his or her identity or remain anonymous. While perpetrators may appear anonymous, however, reports indicate that targets often know who their perpetrators are. And the perpetrators are often friends or, more likely, former friends.

The term "cyberbullying" commonly is used to refer to communications among children and youth. Adults may be involved in cyberbullying, either as bullies or targets, but studies indicate that the majority of those involved in cyberbullying are children and youth.

Bullying and harassment can occur both online and offline. On the playground, bullying may take the form of pushing, hitting, threatening, or other assaultive conduct. On the Internet or on cell phones, bullying comes in the form of speech. Targets of cyberbullying may also be targets of offline bullying. One report found that over 42 percent of youth who reported being cyberbullied also reported being bullied at school.

Because cyberbullying has no clear definition, it is difficult to measure. Lack of an agreed-upon definition also makes it difficult to compare studies or determine trends. According to the Internet Safety Technical Task Force, directed by the Berkman Center for Internet and Society at Harvard University, bullying and harassment by peers are most frequently threats that minors face both online and offline.

All seem to agree that cyberbullying and harassment happens to a significant minority of youth. Bullying appears to be more common than harassment. Sibling-based harassment also occurs, with one study reporting that 30 percent of 7th- through 9th-graders reported online victimization from a non-parent family member.

Some children and youth are involved in cyberbullying as both victims and bullies. A recent study found that 27 percent of girls who were bullied online retaliated back with their own cyberbullying.

Much cyberbullying conduct is typical adolescent behavior, but when it occurs online it is taken to a new level. Insults, harassing, and bullying statements are broadcast to thousands of others in seconds. Once it is out, statements cannot be taken back. Cyberbullying can be devastating to youth and, for some teenagers, can result in tragic endings, such as Megan Meier's suicide.

Unchecked, the problem of cyberbullying likely will only grow worse. We have two bills before us today that take two different approaches to the problem.

H.R. 1966, the "Megan Meier Cyberbullying Prevention Act," addresses the problem by creating a new Federal crime prohibiting communications made with the intent to coerce, intimidate, harass, or cause substantial emotional distress that use electronic means to support severe, repeated, and hostile behavior. The new crime provides for a felony penalty.

We want to do all we can do to protect our children and youth, but we don't want the unintended consequences of converting many of our youth into criminals, particularly felons. The label "felon" lasts a lifetime, and we need to be extremely careful before proceeding down this path.

Finally, as with any attempt to regulate speech, we must be careful not to violate the constitutional right to free speech and due process. So I look forward to hearing what our experts have to say about these concerns.

H.R. 3630, the "Adolescent Web Awareness Requires Education Act," the "AWARE Act," seeks to address the problem of online safety issues for youth, including cyberbullying, through education and prevention. It creates a grant program to be implemented by the Attorney General in accordance with best practices and authorizes $125 million for grants to carry out Internet crime awareness and cyber-crime prevention programs.

While we don't have any bills before us that focus on how technology companies can help with this problem, I am also interested from hearing from our witnesses on this issue. We may need to revisit the immunity portion of section 230 of the "Communications Decency Act" to determine whether the law went too far in providing immunity to service providers who intentionally allow or even encourage cyberbullying and harassment to flourish on their sites.

This is a serious problem, and there is no easy solution. And I appreciate the efforts taken by both the gentlelady from California, Ms. Sánchez, and the gentlelady from Florida, Ms. Wasserman Schultz, to address the problem. And I look forward to hearing from our experts on how we can and should work together to address the problem.

[The bills, H.R. 1966 and H.R. 3630 follow]:

I

111TH CONGRESS
1ST SESSION

H. R. 1966

To amend title 18, United States Code, with respect to cyberbullying.

IN THE HOUSE OF REPRESENTATIVES

APRIL 2, 2009

Ms. LINDA T. SÁNCHEZ of California (for herself, Ms. KAPTUR, Mr. YARMUTH, Ms. ROYBAL-ALLARD, Mrs. CAPPS, Mr. BISHOP of New York, Mr. BRALEY of Iowa, Mr. GRIJALVA, Mr. HARE, Mr. HIGGINS, Mr. CLAY, Mr. SARBANES, Mr. DAVIS of Illinois, Mr. COURTNEY, and Mr. KIRK) introduced the following bill; which was referred to the Committee on the Judiciary

A BILL

To amend title 18, United States Code, with respect to cyberbullying.

Be it enacted by the Senate and House of Representatives of the United States of America in Congress assembled,

SECTION 1. SHORT TITLE.

This Act may be cited as the "Megan Meier Cyberbullying Prevention Act".

SEC. 2. FINDINGS.

Congress finds the following:

(1) Four out of five of United States children aged 2 to 17 live in a home where either they or their parents access the Internet.

(2) Youth who create Internet content and use social networking sites are more likely to be targets of cyberbullying.

(3) Electronic communications provide anonymity to the perpetrator and the potential for widespread public distribution, potentially making them severely dangerous and cruel to youth.

(4) Online victimizations are associated with emotional distress and other psychological problems, including depression.

(5) Cyberbullying can cause psychological harm, including depression; negatively impact academic performance, safety, and the well-being of children in school; force children to change schools; and in some cases lead to extreme violent behavior, including murder and suicide.

(6) Sixty percent of mental health professionals who responded to the Survey of Internet Mental Health Issues report having treated at least one patient with a problematic Internet experience in the previous five years; 54 percent of these clients were 18 years of age or younger.

SEC. 3. CYBERBULLYING.

(a) IN GENERAL.—Chapter 41 of title 18, United States Code, is amended by adding at the end the following:

"§ 881. Cyberbullying

"(a) Whoever transmits in interstate or foreign commerce any communication, with the intent to coerce, intimidate, harass, or cause substantial emotional distress to a person, using electronic means to support severe, repeated, and hostile behavior, shall be fined under this title or imprisoned not more than two years, or both.

"(b) As used in this section—

"(1) the term 'communication' means the electronic transmission, between or among points specified by the user, of information of the user's choosing, without change in the form or content of the information as sent and received; and

"(2) the term 'electronic means' means any equipment dependent on electrical power to access an information service, including email, instant messaging, blogs, websites, telephones, and text messages.".

(b) CLERICAL AMENDMENT.—The table of sections at the beginning of chapter 41 of title 18, United States

Code, is amended by adding at the end the following new item:

"881. Cyberbullying.".

○

I

111TH CONGRESS
1ST SESSION

H. R. 3630

To promote crime awareness and cybercrime prevention initiatives, and for other purposes.

IN THE HOUSE OF REPRESENTATIVES

SEPTEMBER 23, 2009

Ms. WASSERMAN SCHULTZ (for herself and Mr. CULBERSON) introduced the following bill; which was referred to the Committee on the Judiciary

---

A BILL

To promote crime awareness and cybercrime prevention initiatives, and for other purposes.

Be it enacted by the Senate and House of Representatives of the United States of America in Congress assembled,

SECTION 1. SHORT TITLE.

This Act may be cited as the "Adolescent Web Awareness Requires Education Act" or the "AWARE Act".

SEC. 2. GRANT PROGRAM.

(a) AUTHORITY TO MAKE GRANTS.—

(1) IN GENERAL.—Subject to subsection (e)(1), the Attorney General shall make grants to eligible

entities to carry out an Internet crime awareness and cybercrime prevention program.

(2) PERIOD.—A grant under this section shall be for a 2-year period.

(b) APPLICATION.—An eligible entity desiring a grant under this section shall submit an application to the Attorney General, which shall include—

(1) a description of the partnership arrangements, if any, of the eligible entity relating to the activities to be carried out with the grant;

(2) a description of the measurable goals of the eligible entity relating to the activities to be carried out with the grant;

(3) a description of how the Internet crime awareness and cybercrime prevention program of the eligible entity shall achieve the measurable goals described in paragraph (2);

(4) a description of the plan of the eligible entity to continue to implement the Internet crime awareness and cybercrime prevention program after the grant under this section ends;

(5) a description of how funds under the grant may be used and coordinated with Internet crime awareness and cybercrime prevention programs being carried out on the date of enactment of this

Act or other Internet crime awareness and cybercrime prevention programs established with grants under this section;

(6) a description of the target audience under the proposed Internet crime awareness and cybercrime prevention program;

(7) a certification that the eligible entity enforces the operation of measures which prevent the Internet from being used to victimize children if the eligible entity provides Internet access to minors; and

(8) any other information or assurances required by the Attorney General.

(c) PRIORITIZATION.—In making grants under this section, the Attorney General shall give priority to an eligible entity that—

(1) identifies and targets children at-risk of engaging in cybercrimes or becoming crime victims;

(2) works in partnership with the private sector, law enforcement, the philanthropic community, the media, researchers, social services organizations, or other community-based groups;

(3) provides Internet crime awareness and cybercrime prevention programs at no cost to students or schools;

(4) accommodates different languages and language proficiencies;

(5) accommodates differing levels of technological sophistication; or

(6) has a viable plan to sustain the Internet crime awareness and cybercrime prevention program after the grant program ends.

(d) USE OF FUNDS.—An eligible entity may use a grant under this section to—

(1) identify, develop, and implement Internet crime awareness and cybercrime prevention programs, including educational technology, multimedia and interactive applications, online resources, and lesson plans;

(2) provide professional training to elementary and secondary school teachers, administrators, and other staff on crime awareness and cybercrime prevention;

(3) educate parents about teaching their children how to protect themselves from becoming victims of Internet crime;

(4) develop Internet crime awareness and cybercrime prevention programs for children;

(5) train and support peer-driven Internet crime awareness and cybercrime prevention initiatives;

(6) coordinate and fund research initiatives that investigate online risks to children and Internet crime awareness and cybercrime prevention; or

(7) develop and implement public education campaigns to promote awareness of crimes against children on the Internet and the prevention of such crimes.

(e) GRANT GUIDANCE.—

(1) IN GENERAL.—Before making grants under this section, and not later than 1 month after the date on which the study under paragraph (3)(A) is completed, the Attorney General, in consultation with education groups, Internet crime awareness and cybercrime prevention groups, and other relevant experts in the field of new media and child safety, shall issue detailed guidance for the grant program under this section.

(2) CONTENTS OF GUIDANCE.—The grant guidance shall be implemented by the Attorney General in accordance with best practices relating to Internet crime awareness and cybercrime prevention and the

research-based recommendations derived from the study conducted under paragraph (3)(A).

(3) INTERNET CRIME AWARENESS AND CYBERCRIME PREVENTION RESEARCH.—

(A) INITIAL RESEARCH.—The Attorney General shall enter into contracts with 1 or more private companies, government agencies, or nonprofit organizations to complete a study, not later than 6 months after the date of enactment of this Act, regarding—

(i) the nature, prevalence, and quality of Internet crime awareness and cybercrime prevention programs and any evidence-based research conducted relating to the programs;

(ii) findings regarding which children are most at risk of becoming crime victims;

(iii) gaps in Internet crime awareness and cybercrime prevention and youth online risk research; and

(iv) any other area determined appropriate by the Attorney General.

(B) ADDITIONAL RESEARCH.—Subject to the availability of appropriations, the Attorney General shall enter into contracts with private companies, government agencies, or nonprofit organizations to conduct additional research regarding the issues described in subparagraph (A). Any research conducted under this subparagraph shall be included in the reports under subsection (g)(3).

(f) TECHNICAL ASSISTANCE.—The Attorney General shall provide technical assistance to eligible entities that receive a grant under this section, which may include maintaining a Web site to facilitate outreach and communication among the eligible entities that receive a grant under this section.

(g) REPORTS.—

(1) ELIGIBLE ENTITIES.—An eligible entity that receives a grant under this section shall submit to the Attorney General and make public an annual report regarding the activities carried out using funds made available under the grant, which shall include—

(A) a description of how the eligible entity implemented the Internet crime awareness and cybercrime prevention program carried out with the grant;

(B) a detailed description of the audience reached;

(C) an analysis of whether and to what degree the goals for the Internet crime awareness and cybercrime prevention program were met;

(D) an analysis of the challenges, if any, that interfered with achieving the goals described in subparagraph (C);

(E) plans for future Internet crime awareness and cybercrime prevention programs; and

(F) an accounting of the funds used.

(2) COMPILATION OF ANNUAL REPORTS FOR REVISED GRANT GUIDANCE.—The Attorney General shall—

(A) review the report under paragraph (1) submitted by each eligible entity that receives a grant under this section during the first fiscal year for which grants under this section are made; and

(B) not later than 6 months after the date on which all reports described in subparagraph (A) are submitted, modify, as appropriate, the grant guidance based on the reports.

(3) REPORTS TO CONGRESS.—Not later than 27 months after the date on which the Attorney General makes the first grant under this section, and annually thereafter, the Attorney General shall

submit to Congress a report regarding the grant program under this section, which shall include—

(A) a compilation of the information and findings of the annual reports submitted under paragraph (1);

(B) the findings and conclusions of the Attorney General, including findings and conclusions relating to the effectiveness of Internet crime awareness and cybercrime prevention programs carried out using a grant under this section; and

(C) best practices identified by the Attorney General relating to Internet crime awareness and cybercrime prevention.

(h) AUTHORIZATION OF APPROPRIATIONS.—

(1) IN GENERAL.—There is authorized to be appropriated to the Attorney General to carry out this section $25,000,000 for each of fiscal years 2010 through 2014.

(2) LIMITATION.—Of amounts made available to carry out this section, not more than 5 percent shall be available to carry out subsections (e), (f), and (g)(2).

SEC. 3. DEFINITIONS.

In this Act, the following definitions apply:

(1) ELIGIBLE ENTITY.—The term "eligible entity" means—

(A) a partnership between a State educational agency and 1 or more local educational agencies (as those terms are defined in section 9101 of the Elementary and Secondary Education Act of 1965 (20 U.S.C. 7801)) of the State;

(B) a local educational agency;

(C) a nonprofit organization; or

(D) a consortium of elementary schools or secondary schools (as those terms are defined in section 9101 of the Elementary and Secondary Education Act of 1965 (20 U.S.C. 7801)) collaborating with an entity described in subparagraph (A), (B), or (C).

(2) GRANT GUIDANCE.—The term "grant guidance" means the grant guidance issued under section 2(e)(1).

(3) INTERNET CRIME AWARENESS AND CYBERCRIME PREVENTION PROGRAM.—The term "Internet crime awareness and cybercrime prevention program" means an age-appropriate, research-based program that prevents children from becoming the victims of Internet crime by encouraging safe

and responsible use of the Internet, promoting an informed, critical understanding of Internet dangers, and educating children, parents, and communities about how to prevent or respond to problems or dangers related to the Internet or new media.

(4) NEW MEDIA.—The term "new media"—

(A) means emerging digital, computerized, or networked information and communication technologies that often have interactive capabilities; and

(B) includes email, instant messaging, text messaging, Web sites, blogs, interactive gaming, social media, cell phones, and mobile devices.

(5) NONPROFIT.—The term "nonprofit" means an organization that is described in section 501(c) of the Internal Revenue Code of 1986 and exempt from tax under section 501(a) of that Code.

○

Mr. SCOTT. I now recognize the Ranking Member of the Subcommittee, the gentleman from Texas, Judge Gohmert.

Mr. GOHMERT. Thank you, Chairman Scott.

As long as there have been children in this world, there have been bigger, meaner children who pick on them. As a small child, often the smallest in my class, youngest in my class in elementary school and junior high, I certainly know about that and about being picked on by bullies.

But when I was in school, the bully could be found in the lunchroom or the school yard, teasing kids, pushing others, or even taking things from them because they were big enough to do so. Times have changed. Now we have chat rooms, social networking sites, and use terms like "cyberbullying" and "cyberstalking." It appears the school bully has found a new playground.

According to the National Crime Prevention Council, cyberbullying affects nearly half of all American teenagers. Cyberbullies send mean text messages, broadcast insulting or degrading comments on the Internet, and even post pictures of the victim for others to see.

My own family has been bullied on the Internet by political bloggers trying to hurt me and my family because of my political positions. Liberal blogs have called me all kinds of names and made efforts to harass me. Some letters to the editor intended to intimidate and harass have been sent by e-mail. So perhaps this would be a way of stopping that.

But 13-year-old Megan Meier, we know her tragic case in which she committed suicide after being told by a boy she had been talking to on MySpace that the world would be a better place without her. As we know, the boy, "Josh," was really the mother of one of Megan's classmates seeking retribution against Megan for allegedly spreading rumors about the woman's daughter.

Ryan Patrick Halligan, also 13, committed suicide after receiving taunting and insulting messages from his middle school classmates questioning his sexuality.

These tragedies are symptomatic of a much larger problem. Why do our teenagers and even their parents think this is acceptable behavior? What are we teaching our young people in our homes and schools about treating others with respect, as you would want to be treated?

Today we will be examining two bills that seek to address this new issue of cyber harassment. In the first, H.R. 1966, it proposes a new Federal criminal offense for cyberbullying. Under this law, a person could face up to 2 years in Federal prison for sending a communication intended to coerce, intimidate, harass, or cause substantial emotional distress to another person.

This proposal raises several significant concerns, not the least of which is its encroachment on protected speech. The Supreme Court has identified those categories of speech that fall outside the protections of the first amendment, including fighting words, obscenity, or what the court characterizes as, quote, "true threats," unquote.

True threats of bodily harm are not protected. They are already crimes. But statements intended to coerce, intimidate, harass, or cause substantial emotional distress, however unsavory, likely do not fall within the category of true threats.

Moreover, are Federal criminal penalties warranted for cyberbullying? Criminal law is or should be the purview of the States because the Federal Government lacks a general police power. As the Supreme Court noted back in 1903 in *Champion v. Ames*, "To hold that Congress has general police power would be to hold that it may accomplish objects not entrusted to the general government and to defeat the operation of the 10th amendment." And, according to the Congressional Research Service, 26 States have already enacted cyberbullying statutes, the majority of which carry misdemeanor, not felony, penalties.

Unlike cyberstalking crimes, which typically involve a credible threat of harm to the victim, cyberbullying does not. Cyberbullying is characterized as intending embarrassment, annoyance, or humiliation to the victim. This conduct is deplorable, but the question is whether or not it is criminal.

Most cyberbullies are teenagers or middle-school-age children. The legislation proposes sending these young people to Federal prison for embarrassing or humiliating a classmate. In fact, underage cyberbullies tried under this statute would most likely be adjudicated as juveniles and not tried as adults. And since there is no juvenile detention facility in the Federal system, these juveniles would be housed in State or private detention facilities, if at all.

The second bill before us today, H.R. 3630, creates a new grant program within the Justice Department to fund Internet crime awareness and cybercrime prevention programs. But I have to question whether a new grant program is what we really need. A number of organizations with expertise in this area already operate Web sites to combat cyberbullying. The tips and tools offered by these sites are free to parents, teachers, and teens.

H.R. 3630 requires the Justice Department to first undertake a study on the nature, prevalence, and quality of Internet crime awareness and cybercrime prevention programs. Then the Department must consult with education groups, Internet crime awareness, and cybercrime prevention groups and prepare detailed guidance for the grant program. This seems like a burdensome task, when we already have in place guidance from organizations like the National Crime Prevention Council and others.

The question is whether we need to spend another $125 million of Chinese money that we will have to borrow in order to insert the Federal bureaucracy into a problem whose true resolution begins at home. Congress should not try to replace the parent or the teacher.

We are currently involved in a truly bipartisan effort that includes efforts by the ACLU, with the Heritage Foundation and Chairman Scott and I, attempting to begin dismantling the vast overcriminalization under Federal law of between 4,000 and 5,000 Federal crimes.

Consider this: The playground still has bullies. When a bully beats up a smaller student and the smaller student goes home, gets on the Internet and says the playground bully is mean, ugly, and stupid, it is the smaller student victim that has now probably committed a Federal felony under this proposed law.

In our desire to address the problems of the day, Congress all too often legislates without first getting to the bottom about any unintended consequences and potential damages to the Constitution.

What happened to Megan Meier and Ryan Halligan is tragic, is devastating. But Federal legislation does not seem to be the answer. Responsible parenting would be a good answer. Accountability for our actions is the answer. Arming young people with confidence and sense of self-worth to ignore the school Internet bully may be the answer.

Although it is tempting because the proposal before us would allow me to pursue and seek indictment and arrest for mean-spirited liberals who have been exceedingly mean to me and my family, it appears to be another chapter in overcriminalization.

I look forward to the discussion on these issues, and yield back the balance of my time.

Mr. SCOTT. Thank you.

We have two distinguished panels of witnesses here to help us consider the issues today. Our first panel consists of Members of Congress.

The first panelist is the gentlelady from the 39th District of California, Representative Linda Sánchez. She is in her fourth term and is a Member of the Judiciary Committee and the Ways and Means Committee. She is a primary author of H.R. 1966, the "Megan Meier Cyberbullying Prevention Act."

Our next panelist is the gentlelady from the 20th District of Florida, Representative Debbie Wasserman Schultz. She is in her third term and is a Member of the Judiciary Committee and the Appropriations Committee, where she serves as Chair of the Legislative Branch Subcommittee of the Appropriations Committee. She is the lead sponsor of H.R. 3630, the "AWARE Act."

And our final panelist, we expected the gentleman from the Seventh District of Texas, Representative John Culberson, but he was unavoidably detained, and we will have his statement entered into the record.*

Each witness' written statement will be entered in the record in its entirety, so I ask our witnesses to summarize your testimony in 5 minutes or less.

And we will begin with the gentlelady from California.

TESTIMONY OF THE HONORABLE LINDA T. SÁNCHEZ, A REPRESENTATIVE IN CONGRESS FROM THE STATE OF CALIFORNIA

Ms. SÁNCHEZ. Thank you, Mr. Chairman and Ranking Member Gohmert, for allowing me the opportunity to testify today about this piece of legislation. I am pleased to be here talking about the critical issue of child online safety because it is a relatively new form for Congress to be grappling with.

When I was first elected to Congress, I held a series of meetings with local school superintendents and law enforcement leaders to learn more about the challenges that they face in keeping kids in school and on the right track to becoming productive citizens. And,

*Due to unforeseen events prior to the hearing, Mr. Culberson did not submit a statement to the Subcommittee.

unfortunately, I heard a recurring theme during this series of meetings, and that is that bullying isn't a harmless prank or some kind of right of passage; it is dangerous, both physically and mentally, for students.

Bullying leads to things like poor school performance, absences from school, or even dropping out of school altogether. The prospect of assault and harassment can lead a child to join a gang for protection. Not only can bullying cause physical injuries in the form of wounds, bruises, and broken bones, but it can also lead to depression and even suicide.

That is why I have been working to change Federal law so that schools can use Federal funds to address and prevent bullying and harassment. But over the last several years, I have learned that that approach isn't going to be enough, because bullying has gone electronic. It occurs in text messages and G-chat, on Facebook and MySpace, on cell phones and on the Internet. This literally means that kids can be bullied any hour of the day and night and even in their own homes, which is a marked contrast to the bullies of yesterday that could only bully on the playground.

Today's kids are so wired into their electronic social networks that they type more messages than they speak each day. Their virtual world is more real to them than the so-called "real world" is. For those of us over 30, this can be difficult to comprehend, so I want to give you an example to illustrate the problem.

Imagine, if you would, in our day when we went to school, a student brought out a jumbo-size TV into the school quad and played for the entire student body a videotape in which he threatened and harassed a second student. By the end of the day, everyone—and I mean everyone—would have seen or heard about it. Well, that is exactly what cyberbullying is.

Because of the anonymity and deception in the Internet, this form of bullying is particularly dangerous. If Bobby posts a video—and I don't mean the Chairman—on his Facebook page that harasses and threatens to rape and kill Ashley, that video isn't private. It is not buried on Bobby's profile page somewhere. It is public. It appears when any of Bobby's Facebook friends log in, right up there in front of their homepage so they can't miss it. And this story isn't just hypothetical. It happened to a brave young woman named Hail Ketchum-Wiggins, who lives in southern California near my congressional district.

Similar bullying incidents are happening every day to young people across our Nation. Cyberbullying is always mean, ill-mannered, and cruel, but some cyberbullying is so harmful that it rises to the level of criminal behavior.

My bill, the "Megan Meier Cyberbullying Prevention Act," is named to honor a young woman who was a victim of such criminal behavior. Three years ago, 13-year-old Megan Meier of Missouri hanged herself after being tormented and harassed by her 15-year-old MySpace friend "Josh." Josh told her, among other things, "The world would be better off without you."

Eventually, Megan's family learned that "Josh" was really a creation of Lori Drew, the parent of one of her classmates. However, local prosecutors in Missouri couldn't bring charges against Lori Drew because, at the time, Missouri had no law to punish that kind of cruelty. A Federal prosecutor in a similar bind got creative and charged Drew with computer fraud. And even though a jury convicted her, a judge through out the conviction. The result is that Drew, an adult and one who should have been setting an example of good behavior, will never be punished for her outrageous behavior toward her 13-year-old victim, Megan.

These are just a few brief examples of why Congress needs to address new crimes like cyberbullying. Words that didn't even exist a couple years ago, including "sexting" and "textual harassment," describe the new ways that people use technology to hurt, harass, and humiliate others. When these behaviors become serious, repeated, and hostile, we can no longer ignore them and turn a blind aye.

While Missouri has since enacted a cyberbullying statute, the children of other States are waiting for Congress to act. That is why I am grateful that the Committee is considering the "Megan Meier Cyberbullying Prevention Act."

Before I conclude, I do want to acknowledge how difficult it is to craft a prohibition on cyberbullying that is consistent with the Constitution. But I believe that, working together for the sake of our children, we can and must do so.

The Supreme Court has already recognized that some regulation of speech is consistent with the first amendment. For example, the Court has approved restrictions on true threats, obscenities, and some commercial speech. But it has been more hostile to attempts to limit political speech.

I don't intend anything in the "Megan Meier Cyberbullying Prevention Act" to override Supreme Court jurisprudence. Instead, I want the law to be able to distinguish between an annoying chain mail, a righteously angry political blog post, or a miffed text to an ex-boyfriend, all of which should remain legal. But serious, repeated, and hostile communications made with the intent to harm are different. When the latter rises to a criminal level, as it did in the case of Lori Drew, prosecutors should have a tool at their disposal to allow them to punish the perpetrator.

I believe that we can protect our right to free speech and protect victims of cyberbullying at the same time. And I look forward to working with my colleagues on both sides of the aisle to do so. I thank you for the opportunity to testify today and hope that you will join me in supporting that legislation.

[The prepared statement of Ms. Sánchez follows:]

PREPARED STATEMENT OF THE HONORABLE LINDA T. SÁNCHEZ, A REPRESENTATIVE IN CONGRESS FROM THE STATE OF CALIFORNIA

Megan Meier Cyberbullying Prevention Act
Rep. Linda T. Sánchez
September 30, 2009

Good afternoon. Chairman Scott and Ranking Member Gohmert, thank you so much for allowing me the opportunity to testify today about this very important legislation.

I am so pleased to be here to discuss the critical issue of child online safety.

When I was first elected to Congress, I held a series of meetings with local school superintendents and law enforcement leaders to learn more about the challenges they face in helping to keep our children safe and on the right track.

I heard a recurring theme—that bullying is not a harmless prank or rite of passage. It is dangerous, both physically and mentally.

Bullying can lead to poor school performance, more absences, or even dropping out of school altogether.

The prospect of assault and harassment can lead a child to join a gang for protection. Not only can bullying cause physical injuries, including cuts, bruises, and broken bones, but it can also lead to depression, and even suicide.

This is why I have been working to change federal law so that schools can use federal funds to address and prevent bullying and harassment.

But, over the last several years, I have learned that this approach isn't enough.

Bullying has gone electronic. It occurs in text messages and G-Chat; on Facebook and MySpace; on cell phones and the internet.

This literally means that kids can be bullied any hour of the day or night and **even in their own homes**.

Today's kids are so wired into their electronic social networks that they type more messages than they speak each day. Their virtual world is more **real** to them than the so-called real world.

For those of us over 30, this can be difficult to comprehend. Let me give you an example to illustrate the problem.

Imagine if, in our day, a student brought a big TV out to the quad and played for the entire student body a video tape in which he threatened and harassed a second student. By the end of the day, everyone, and I mean everyone, would have seen or heard about it.

Well, that's exactly what cyberbullying is. Because of the anonymity and deception the internet allows, this form of bullying particularly dangerous.

If Bobby posts a video on his Facebook page that harasses and threatens to rape and kill Ashley, that video isn't private. It's not buried on Bobby's profile page somewhere.

It's public. It appears when any of Bobby's Facebook friends log in—right there up front on their home page, so they can't miss it.

This story isn't just a hypothetical. It happened to a brave young woman named Hail Ketchum-Wiggins, who lives in Southern California, near my Congressional district.

And similar bullying incidents are happening every day to young people across our nation.

Cyberbullying is always mean, ill mannered, and cruel. But some cyberbullying is so harmful that it rises to the level of criminal behavior.

My bill, the Megan Meier Cyberbullying Prevention Act, is named to honor a young woman who was the victim of just such criminal behavior.

Three years ago, 13-year-old Megan Meier of Missouri hung herself after being tormented and harassed by her 15-year-old MySpace friend "Josh." 'Josh" told her, among other things, "The world would be better off without you."

Eventually, Megan's family learned that "Josh" was really a creation of Lori Drew.

Local prosecutors in Missouri couldn't bring charges against Lori Drew because, at the time, Missouri had no law to punish such cruelty.

A federal prosecutor, in a similar bind, got creative and charged Drew with computer fraud. Even though the jury convicted her, the judge threw out the conviction.

The result is that Drew, an adult, and one who should have been setting an example of good behavior, will never be punished for her outrageous behavior toward her 13-year-old victim, Megan.

These are just brief examples of why Congress needs to address new crimes like cyberbullying.

Words that didn't exist just a couple of years ago, including "sexting," and "textual harassment," describe the new ways people use technology to hurt, harass, and humiliate each other. When these behaviors become serious, repeated, and hostile, we can no longer ignore them.

While Missouri has since enacted a cyberbullying statute, the children of other states are waiting for Congress to act. That is why I am grateful that the Committee is considering the Megan Meier Cyberbullying Prevention Act.

Before I conclude, I want to acknowledge how difficult it will be to craft a prohibition on cyberbullying that is consistent with the Constitution. But I also believe that working together for our children, we can and must do so.

The Supreme Court has already recognized that some regulation of speech is consistent with the First Amendment. For example, the Court has approved restrictions on true threats, obscenities, and some commercial speech. But is has been more hostile to attempts to limit political speech.

I do not intend anything in the Megan Meier Cyberbullying Prevention Act to override Supreme Court jurisprudence.

Instead, I want the law to be able to distinguish between an annoying chain email, a righteously angry political blog post, or a miffed text to an ex-boyfriend—all of which are and should remain legal; and serious, repeated, and hostile communications made with the intent to harm.

When the latter rises to a criminal level, as it did in the case of Lori Drew, prosecutors should have a tool at their disposal to allow them to punish the perpetrator.

I believe that we can protect our right to free speech **and** victims of cyberbullying at the same time.

I look forward to working with colleagues on both sides of the aisle to do so.

I thank you for the opportunity to testify today and hope that you will all join me in supporting this legislation.

Mr. SCOTT. Thank you.
Ms. Wasserman Schultz?

TESTIMONY OF THE HONORABLE DEBBIE WASSERMAN SCHULTZ, A REPRESENTATIVE IN CONGRESS FROM THE STATE OF FLORIDA

Ms. WASSERMAN SCHULTZ. Thank you, Chairman Scott and Ranking Member Gohmert and distinguished Members of the Committee, for allowing me to testify today beside my friend and fellow Committee colleague, Representative Linda Sánchez. And I want to acknowledge my colleague, Representative John Culberson, who has taken ill and was not able to join us today.

It is always an honor to appear before this Subcommittee, and I am pleased that we continue to make protecting children online a high priority.

You know, Mr. Chairman, as proud as I am to represent south Florida in the House of Representatives, the job closest to my heart is being a mother to my 10-year-old twins and my 6-year-old daughter. And, as one of only a handful of mothers with young children in Congress—and Representative Sánchez has recently joined our ranks, and we welcome her and congratulate her on that—I can assure you that we have no higher priority than keeping our children safe from harm.

Now, for me, I approach today's topic as a Web-savvy mom with Web-savvy kids. In fact, as of yesterday, literally, my 6-year-old daughter now has an e-mail address which she uses on her iPod Touch—with strong parental control software fully engaged, I might add. Clearly, parents and teachers already know that our children are growing up in a completely different world than we did, as Representative Sánchez acknowledged.

The Internet is a wonderful tool, but it has also become a pathway for risky behavior. The same Internet that helps our children create, study, and explore the world also enables minors to post nude photos online or text them to friends. The same Internet that allows children to organize clubs and volunteer for after-school activities also provides a way for children to harass their fellow students relentlessly, anonymously, publicly, and after the school day has long ended.

As legislators, we have to get real. We must accept that our kids spend more time online than in front of the television. We have to own up to the fact that 89 percent of teenagers have profiles on social networking sites like MySpace and Facebook. We must understand that nearly four in 10 kids have used the Internet to make fun of or post lies about their fellow students. We must understand that we live in an era when four out of five teenagers have cell phones, most of which have cameras. And we must know that more than one in five teenagers admit to sexting nude photos of themselves to peers.

These behaviors, often done on impulse or in boredom, have devastating real-life consequences. This May, I had the honor of meeting Cynthia Logan, a young mother from Ohio. She told me her story, and it truly broke my heart.

Her daughter, Jesse, was only 18 years old when she sent nude photos of herself to her boyfriend. After the young couple broke up, the ex-boyfriend sent them to other high school girls all over the school. They called Jesse names I can't repeat in this hearing. They passed around her pictures as casually as they would notes in a classroom. And they made Jesse's life a living hell. What began as a private communication turned into a public humiliation. Jesse became miserable and depressed. She eventually took her own life.

Sadly, her case is not unique. Megan Meier, the young teen from Missouri that is the namesake of Congresswoman Sánchez's legislation, also committed suicide after being bullied online. It is not surprising that researchers at the Yale School of Medicine have found significant links between bullying and suicide.

There are other dire consequences to these behaviors. An 18-year-old boy in my own home State of Florida was convicted on child pornography charges for sexted photos. He must now register as a sex offender for the rest of his life.

So what do we do about it? There is no one answer or one silver bullet, but we can either continue to shut our eyes to the reality or we can tackle this problem head-on.

I believe that we must usher in a new era of Internet safety education and cybercrime awareness. We must teach children how to be good cyber citizens. Unfortunately, most parents and most teachers don't feel comfortable teaching kids how to be safe online. This means most children receive no training whatsoever in the safe, smart, and responsible use of the Internet. I, myself, have held three Internet safety town halls in my district. But as individuals and parents, we can't do this alone. We need a consistent and national approach.

Last week, with Congressman Culberson, I was proud to introduce H.R. 3630, the "Adolescent Web Awareness Requires Education Act," or the "AWARE Act." Our bill will establish a competitive grant program so that nonprofit Internet safety organizations can work together with schools and communities to educate students, teachers, and parents about these online dangers.

Our bill authorizes up to $125 million over 5 years to establish age-appropriate, research-based programs that will encourage the safe, smart, and responsible use of the Internet and teach cybercrime awareness and digital literacy in the new media to our children.

Education is important because it helps teach both parents and children how to act in all kinds of real-life situations. Education is vital because it can reinforce new norms between students. Education gives children lessons, teaches skills, and builds strength that can last a lifetime.

We can teach children to treat their fellow students the same way online that they would in person. We can teach them not to bully or harass their peers and how to report dangerous our threatening activity when they see it. We can teach them not to post inappropriate material about themselves or others. We can teach them about privacy settings and about the risks of talking to strangers or posting personal information online. We can teach them that what they put online stays online. And we can teach them that the minute they hit that send button, they not only lose control over where their photos go next, they can also lose control of their future.

We can and we must teach children how to be safe on the Web. Jesse Logan's death was a tragedy, but it also is a powerful reminder about the lives that we can save. Knowledge truly is power, and with the "AWARE Act," it is my hope that we make knowledge our children's first line of defense.

Thank you.

[The prepared statement of Ms. Wasserman Schultz follows:]

PREPARED STATEMENT OF THE HONORABLE DEBBIE WASSERMAN SCHULTZ, A REPRESENTATIVE IN CONGRESS FROM THE STATE OF FLORIDA

Testimony before the House Judiciary Committee
Subcommittee on Crime, Terrorism, and Homeland Security
September 30, 2009
Rep. Debbie Wasserman Schultz

Thank you, Chairman Scott, Ranking Member Gohmert, and distinguished Members of the Subcommittee, for allowing me to testify today beside my friend and fellow committee colleague, Representative Linda Sanchez, and my friend and lead Republican co-sponsor, Representative John Culberson. It is always an honor to appear before this Committee, and I am pleased that we continue to make protecting children online a high priority.

As proud as I am to represent South Florida in the House of Representatives, the job closest to my heart is being a mother to my ten-year-old twins and six-year-old daughter. As one of only a handful of mothers with young children in Congress, I can assure you that I have no higher priority than keeping our children safe from harm. I approach today's topic as a web-savvy mom with web-savvy kids. In fact, as of yesterday, my six-year-old daughter has an email address, which she uses on her iPod Touch.

Parents and teachers already know that our children are growing up in a completely different world than we did. The Internet is a wonderful tool, but it has also become an pathway for risky behavior. The same Internet that helps our children create, study, and explore the world also enables minors to post nude photos online or text them to friends. The same Internet that allows children to organize clubs and volunteer for after-school activities also provides a way for children to harass their fellow students relentlessly, anonymously, publicly, and after the school day has long ended.

As legislators, we have to get real. We must accept that our kids spend more time online than in front of the television.[1] We have to own up to the fact that 89 percent of teenagers have profiles on social networking sites like MySpace and Facebook.[2] We must understand that nearly four in ten kids have used the Internet to make fun of, or post lies about, their fellow students.[3] We must understand we live in an era when four out of five teenagers have cell phones -- most of which

---

1 Alex Mindlin, *Preferring the Web Over Watching TV*, N.Y. Times, Aug. 25, 2008, at C3 (reporting a survey that found that 83 percent of children between the ages of 10 and 14 spend more than an hour on the Internet each day, while only 68 percent of the same group spent that much time in front of the television.)

2 Hearing Testimony of Judi Westberg Warren, Web Wise Kids, House Committee on the Judiciary, Subcommittee on Crime, Terrorism, and Homeland Security, September 30, 2009, at 2.

3 Common Sense Media, *Is Social Networking Changing Childhood? A National Poll*, available at http://www.commonsensemedia.org/sites/default/files/Social%20Networking%20Poll%20Summary%20Results.pdf, at 6. The poll, conducted between May 28, 2009, and June 5, 2009, showed that 37 percent of respondents between the ages of 13 and 18 admitted to making fun of other students online and another 16 percent admitted to posting lies about other people.

have cameras.[4] And we must know that more than one in five teenagers admit to "sexting" nude photos of themselves to peers.[5]

These behaviors, often done on impulse or in boredom, have devastating, real-life consequences. This May, I had the honor of meeting Cynthia Logan, a young mother from Ohio. She told me her story, and it broke my heart. Her daughter, Jesse, was only 18 years old when she sent nude photos of herself to her boyfriend. After the young couple broke up, the ex-boyfriend sent them to other high school girls. They called Jesse names I can't repeat in this hearing. They passed around her pictures as casually as they would notes in a classroom. They made Jesse's life a living hell. What began as a private communication turned into a *public humiliation*. Jesse became miserable and depressed. She eventually took her own life.

Sadly, Jesse's case is not unique. Megan Meier, the young teen from Missouri who is the namesake of Congresswoman Sanchez' legislation, also committed suicide after being bullied online. It is not surprising that researchers at the Yale School of Medicine have found significant links between bullying and suicide.[6]

There are other dire consequences to these behaviors. An 18-year-old boy in my own home state of Florida was convicted on child pornography charges for "sexted" photos. He must now register as a sex offender for the rest of his life.[7]

So, what do we do about it? There is no "one answer" – there is no "silver bullet." But we can either continue to shut our eyes to the reality, or we can tackle this problem head-on. I believe we must usher in a new era of Internet safety education and cyber-crime awareness. Instead of preventing our children from using the Internet, or criminalizing speech online that would be permissible on the playground, we must instead teach children how to be good cyber-citizens.

---

[4] *See* Westberg Warren testimony, *supra*, at 2. *See also* Nielsen Poll: "Mobile Kids Insights: Profiling the Youngest Mobile Audience," *available at http://en-us.nielsen.com/etc/medialib/nielsen_dotcom/en_us/documents/pdf/fact_sheets.Par.78796.File.dat/Nielsen%20Mobile%20Kids%20Fact%20Sheet_12-08.pdf*.

[5] A Chicago based trend analyst firm called Teenage Research Unlimited recently surveyed 1200 students about "sexting." One out of every five students told researchers they had used their cell phones to send sexy or nude photos of themselves. *Keagan Harsha (2009-01-03). "Is Your Child "Sexting"?". WCAX-TV.* http://www.wcax.com/Global/story.asp?S=9612361&nav=menu183_2 (retrieved January 14, 2009). Additionally, in the Common Sense Media poll, *supra* note 3 at 6, 13 percent of respondents between the ages of 13 and 18 admitted sending or posting naked or semi-naked photos of themselves or others online. This poll also shows that parents are out of touch with this behavior, as only 2 percent of parents polled believe their children were posting or sending such photos. *Id.*

[6] Berin Szoka & Adam Thierer, *Cyberbullying Legislation: Why Education is Preferable to Regulation*, Progress on Point, Volume 16, Issue 12 (June 2009), at 2 (citing *Bullying and Being Bullied Linked to Suicide in Children, Review of Studies Suggests*, ScienceDaily, July 19, 2008, *available at* www.sciencedaily.com/releases/2008/07/080717170428.htm) .

[7] Deborah Feyerick and Sheila Steffen, *'Sexting' Lands Teen on Sex Offender List*, CNN American Morning, April 8, 2009, *available at* http://www.cnn.com/2009/CRIME/04/07/sexting.busts/index.html.

Unfortunately, most parents and most teachers don't feel comfortable teaching kids how to be safe online.[8] This means most children receive no training in the safe, smart, and responsible use of the Internet. I myself have held three Internet safety town halls in my District, but as individuals and parents, we can't do this alone. We need a consistent, national approach.

Last week, with Congressman Culberson, I was proud to introduce H.R. 3630, the Adolescent Web Awareness Requires Education Act, or the AWARE Act. Our bill will establish a competitive grant program so that non-profit Internet safety organizations can work together with schools and communities to educate students, teachers and parents about these online dangers. Our bill authorizes up to $125 million over five years to establish age-appropriate, research-based programs that will encourage the safe, smart, and responsible use of the Internet and teach cyber-crime awareness and digital literacy in the new media to our children.

Education is important because it helps teach both parents and children how to act in all kinds of real-life situations. Education is vital because it can reinforce new norms between students. Education gives children lessons, teaches skills, and builds strength that can last a lifetime. We can teach children to treat their fellow students the same way online that they would in person. We can teach them not to bully or harass their peers, and how to report dangerous or threatening activity when they see it. We can teach them not to post inappropriate material about themselves or others. We can teach them about privacy settings and about the risks of talking to strangers or posting personal information online. We can teach them that what they put online, stays online. We can teach them that the minute they hit send, they not only lose control over where their photos go next, they can also lose control of their future.

We can teach children how to be safe on the Web.

Jesse Logan's death was a tragedy, but it is also a powerful reminder about the lives we can save. Knowledge is power – and, with the AWARE Act, it is my hope that we make knowledge our children's first line of defense.

Thank you.

[8] *See* Schools Need Training to Build a Safe Net, *available at* http://www.edtechpolicy.org/NCSA/Archived/21stCenturyConnectinos.pdf. According to the survey, 75 percent of teachers don't feel comfortable discussing cyber-bullying and less than 32 percent are comfortable giving guidance on how to be safe in an online environment, including social networking and online predators.

Mr. SCOTT. Thank you very much.

Do you have questions for the witnesses?

Mr. GOHMERT. No.

Mr. SCOTT. We want to thank you for your testimony, and we are going to go on with the other witnesses. Thank you very much.

If the other witnesses will come forward.

Our second panel of witnesses consists of five distinguished witnesses.

Our first panelist will be professor Robert O'Neil. In 1990, he founded the Thomas Jefferson Center for the Protection of Free Expression and was director until 2007. Though officially a professor emeritus from the University of Virginia, he continues to teach a first amendment clinic. He is the author of several books, including "Free Speech in the College Community," "The First Amendment and Civil Liability," and "Academic Freedom in the Wired World."

Our next panelist is Judi Westberg Warren. Since 2004, she has served as president of Web Wise Kids, a national nonprofit organization that implements educational programs to help our youth stay online safely. She serves on numerous committees, including the Congressional Internet Caucus Advisory Committee and the Internet Safety Advisory Board for the Attorney General of Virginia.

Our next witness is Harvey Silverglate. He is the counsel to the Boston law firm of Zalkind, Rodriguez, Lunt & Duncan, LLP, specializing in criminal defense, civil liberties and academic freedom, and student rights law. He currently serves as an adjunct professor with the Cato Institute and is speaking on its behalf today.

Our next panelist is Nancy Willard. She is the director of the Center for Safe and Responsible Internet Use and has degrees in special education and the law. She is author of two books, "Cyberbullying and Cyberthreats: Responding to the Challenge of Online Social Cruelty, Threats, and Distress;" and "Cyber-Safe Kids, Cyber-Savvy Teens: Helping Young People Use the Internet Safety and Responsibly."

And our final panelist is John Palfrey, professor of law and vice dean for library and information resources at Harvard Law School. He is the co-author of "Born Digital: Understanding the First Generation of Digital Natives" and also "Access Denied: The Practice and Politics of Internet Filtering." He recently chaired the Internet Safety Technical Task Force directed by the Berkman Center for Internet and Society at Harvard University.

Each of the witnesses' written statements will be entered into the record in its entirety. And I would ask each of our witnesses to summarize your testimony in 5 minutes or less.

And to help you, there is a timing device on the table. It will start off green, will go to yellow when there is 1 minute remaining, and will turn red when your 5 minutes have expired.

Professor O'Neil, it is good to see you again.

TESTIMONY OF ROBERT M. O'NEIL, LAW PROFESSOR EMERITUS, UNIVERSITY OF VIRGINIA, CHARLOTTESVILLE, VA

Mr. O'NEIL. Thank you, Mr. Chairman and Representative Gohmert. I am delighted and honored to have an opportunity to come to discuss with you a vital but also an exceedingly difficult issue of national policy. This is my 47th year of teaching constitutional law, free speech, and press, and this is one of the toughest issues I think I have ever encountered.

Of those 47 years, I spent much of the last 25 teaching at the University of Virginia and, most recently, this past spring, at the University of Texas. So, from those experiences, nearly a half-century, I had hoped to share four or five fairly basic points, which are more fully developed in the written statement that I had filed.

First, it seems to me this issue has recently acquired a new kind of urgency, in part because of the graphic, sometimes cruel, brutal, and devastating experiences that the two earlier witnesses described so graphically and vividly. For me, as the grandfather of an Internet-savvy young lady who just turned 13, it is hard to avoid the potentially personal impact of such transgressions.

It also acquires an urgency because, within the past month, the Federal district judge in southern California, by dismissing the charges against Lori Drew under the "Computer Fraud and Abuse Act," essentially left Federal prosecutors with no viable recourse against even the most cruel form, the most extreme form of cyberbullying.

Obviously, as Representative Gohmert pointed out earlier, any solution this Subcommittee or the full Committee or the Congress may craft must be compatible with the first amendment to the Constitution, must recognize the protections of free speech and press.

Obviously, that requires finding some exception to those protections, the more urgent in this country because uniquely we, in the United States, and our courts presume that speech is protected until and unless it is shown to fall within one of several rather narrowly defined exceptions. Several exceptions have been suggested in this context—incitement, defamation, deception, true threats, invasion of privacy, fighting words—but for one reason or another, none of those exceptions really seems to be viable in this context.

The one that potentially works is the one on which H.R. 1966 is premised, and that is intentional infliction of emotional distress. It is not a perfect fit, but that is a well-recognized tort remedy which has never been thought to violate or abridge free speech or free press.

It hasn't traditionally been applied in the criminal context, and that is one of the variations that requires consideration in this instance. But, for a whole lot of reasons, it seems to me that intentional infliction of emotional distress is by far the most promising of the various and potentially available exceptions to first amendment protection.

It seems to me that H.R. 1966 is certainly on the right track. It is a very promising approach to this problem. I would, however, respectfully suggest consideration of three ways in which 1966 might be strengthened: The first would be to look at all possible types of intent which ought to be potentially punishable. The second would be to require proof that a particular person or victim has been targeted or singled out for special attention as a critical element of cyberbullying.

The third is to require some evidence of impact or effect. In most cases, this would not be anything nearly as drastic as Megan Meier's suicide. But I would suspect that, in a viable Federal prosecution, there would be evidence at least of time lost from school, of physical or other illness, consequences to the family, and so on.

So I would respectfully urge consideration by the Subcommittee of possibly strengthening H.R. 1966 in those three respects.

Thank you. I would be happy to answer questions, but I very much appreciate this opportunity.

[The prepared statement of Mr. O'Neil follows:]

PREPARED STATEMENT OF ROBERT M. O'NEIL

Testimony of

Robert M. O'Neil

Director, Thomas Jefferson Center for the
Protection of Free Expression

Charlottesville, Virginia

September 30, 2009

House of Representatives Judiciary Committee
Subcommittee on Crime, Terrorism and Homeland Security

Hearing on

H.R. 1966 and H.R. 3630

Mr. Chairman and members of the Subcommittee, let me first express my deep appreciation for the opportunity you have given me to address this vital issue of national policy. I am Robert O'Neil, Director of the Thomas Jefferson Center for the Protection of Free Expression, a non-partisan, non-profit organization in Charlottesville, Virginia. Among our Trustees are Norman Dorsen, Brit Hume and Sissy Spacek, though I should make clear that time constraints prevented me from seeking the Board's concurrence to the testimony I will offer here. Our Center files amicus curiae briefs in a host of free speech and free press cases, and I have been privileged to testify before Congressional committees on issues as varied as campaign finance reform and expression on the National Mall and in national parks.

As a lifelong specialist in constitutional law, I am in my forty-sixth year of teaching about the First Amendment, most recently for twenty five years at the University of Virginia and last semester at the University of Texas. I have written on a variety of First Amendment issues in both legal and general publications.

The issue before you this afternoon has a special urgency, which I share. Not only is cyber bullying a most venal and intolerable abuse of the freedom of speech that Internet users enjoy but, because of new and vastly different technologies, cyber bullying has eluded sanctions that protect potential victims of more traditional abuses such as stalking, threats and the like. And because of the interstate nature of such abuses, new federal legislation is critically needed. This subcommittee is clearly the optimal source of such sanctions. I applaud your initiative in addressing this challenge. I might add that the First Amendment and media communities seem quite ready, despite their firm commitment to free speech, to support such legislation if it recognizes and protects expressive interests.

Recent events only heighten that sense of urgency. When a federal district judge several weeks ago set aside the conviction of the most celebrated cyber bully in the case involving the harassment of Megan Meier, that action was clearly proper. Despite the creativity of those who charged the perpetrator, Lori Drew, her conviction stretched the Computer Fraud and Abuse Act well beyond its proper scope. That statute is critically needed to address a host of potential electronic abuses – but not this one. Thus Judge Wu did the cause a favor by making clear the need for an Act of Congress that more precisely meets the need posed by cyber bullying.

The challenge in this, as in so many situations that involve dangerous or harmful expression, is to separate speech that is constitutionally protected from speech that may be punished consistent with the First Amendment. That task is singularly difficult in the United States, since we are the only developed nation that steadfastly refuses to criminalize "hate speech." Indeed, the Supreme Court has made clear that even hateful and deeply hurtful words are presumptively entitled to First Amendment protection – a view that even neighbors and allies as near as Canada do not share. Uniquely, our courts insist that speech even of the most venal sort may be punished only if it falls within one of the few clearly defined exceptions to the First Amendment. But the key word here is "presumptively." And the challenge facing us is to identify possible exceptions that might warrant imposing federal penalties on cyber bulling despite the presumption of protection. I would not have agreed to join you this afternoon if I did not believe that can and should be done.

Several possibilities have been suggested, though closer scrutiny reveals that most of them are no more helpful than the Computer Fraud and Abuse Act. First, let's consider threats. The Supreme Court in the *Watts* case strongly implied (and lower federal courts regularly assume) that "true threats" may be punished consistent with the First Amendment, though there are differences in the scope of that exception. Congress adopted over a decade ago a law that criminalizes electronic threats; though it has been infrequently applied, First Amendment scholars assume as I do that it comports with First Amendment constraints. Though some messages that constitute cyber bullying might be criminalized under the electronic threat statute, many others would probably not meet the Supreme Court's properly rigorous definition of "threat." Thus, despite partial help from this source, we should explore other possible sources.

We face similar limitations with the doctrine of "incitement," which forty years ago the Supreme Court recognized in the *Brandenburg* case as a permissible limit on free speech. But in so doing, the Justices imposed conditions that would be virtually impossible to meet in a cyber bulling case – that the targeted speech must pose a direct threat of "imminent lawless action" with a high probability such action would promptly ensue. However grave the danger that cyber bullying ultimately poses for its victims and their families, meeting the incitement standard would be virtually impossible.

The Supreme Court has also recognized a First Amendment exception for "fighting words" – language so provocative that it would almost certainly trigger immediate violence from the person to whom it is directed. But the major problem here is that "fighting words" must occur in a face-to-face situation. Even an inflammatory telephone message probably would not be covered. An Internet message, even addressed to a named person, could not possibly meet the properly high standards that must be met in order to convict a speaker for uttering fighting words.

Another recognized exception – this one for libel and slander – yields no greater promise. Although a victim of cyber bullying would almost certainly be a non-public figure and thus unhampered by the *New York Times* privilege and other exceptions the Supreme Court has crafted, criminal sanctions for defamatory statements would be highly suspect – even if the messages sent by a cyber bully could be meaningfully subjected to the kind of truth/falsehood analysis that a libel claim would demand. Once again, a well recognized exception fails to offer helpful guidance here. Much the same could be said for "invasion of privacy," the constitutional status of which is less clear than defamation, and the applicability of which here also seems doubtful.

Only one other promising path remains – intentional infliction of emotional distress. Clearly this long recognized tort claim fits the facts; if a cyber bully's heinous messages do not constitute such an intentional act, it would be hard to find a closer match. There are, however, several possible obstacles along that path. For one, the Supreme Court has not been especially friendly to this cause of action. When the late Reverend Jerry Falwell sued Hustler Magazine publisher Larry Flynt, the Justices startled First Amendment observers by reversing the intentional infliction claim (the only surviving issue on which Falwell had prevailed) on First Amendment grounds.

There were, however, special circumstances in that case that might not encumber a cyber bullying charge. Most notable was the highly visible public figure status of Reverend Falwell, which clearly barred a libel claim for the offending Hustler copy. His status also caused the majority to express grave doubts about the viability of an intentional infliction claim tied, as it had been, to a *New York Times*-barred libel suit. (These doubts arose from the special circumstances of the case. Although the Justices seemed to leave open the possibility of an intentional infliction claim that could meet the "actual malice" standard of the *Times* case, the evidence so clearly established such animus on Flynt's and Hustler's part that the ruling seemed to foreclose even that remote prospect if the plaintiff was a public figure.) So let's assume for the moment that the *Falwell/Hustler* case does not so clearly discredit intentional infliction that we should abandon this theory when it comes to cyber bullying.

There is at least one other potential obstacle. Intentional infliction has historically been the accepted basis for a civil tort remedy. In the civil context, the prototype case is familiar: As a cruel joke or hoax one person sends what in the old days would have been a telegram (today an e-mail) expressing feigned condolences upon the death of the recipient's father or mother or other close relative, when in fact the person mentioned is in perfect health. The victim of such a vicious prank may sue for intentional infliction, as many have over the years. A damage award in such a case has never been assumed to abridge First Amendment freedoms – as the Justices noted somewhat grudgingly in the *Falwell/Hustler* case before turning to the public figure problem. While the precise basis for such an exception has not been fully defined, a close analogy to fraud, deceit, inducement and other expression that is never deemed worthy of constitutional protection naturally arises. So we may assume that in its traditional civil setting, a remedy for infliction of emotional distress should pass muster.

The ultimate question we now face is how differently a criminal sanction for such abusive speech would be viewed. I am unaware of any other context in which intentional infliction has been made unlawful or criminal penalties have been seriously considered. Those states that have already passed cyber bullying laws seem to assume the validity of such sanctions, and although at least one such case was recently filed under the Missouri statute, there seems to have been no ruling on the constitutional issue there or elsewhere. So let us assume that, in the absence of any judgment to the contrary, a case can be made for applying this historically accepted civil tort remedy in a criminal setting.

Given the several uncertainties I have noted, and clear recognition that we are charting new legal terrain, let me strongly urge consideration of two conditions I believe would enhance the prospect for a cyber bullying criminal statute. The first would be to require proof not only of the type of vicious intent that is prescribed by the draft now before this committee, but to add a more specific element of "targeting" a particular victim as the object of that intent and of the messages that constitute the charged offense. Such a requirement has proved helpful in the "true threat" context, and should be equally persuasive here as well. While I could not say that omitting such a condition would cause a cyber bullying statute to fail, its inclusion would seem to me not only prudent but also relatively easy for prosecutors to satisfy.

The other element may be a bit more of a challenge, but I do urge its careful consideration. Civil suits for intentional infliction have been greatly enhanced by proof of impact or effect. Including such a requirement in a federal cyber bulling law would in my view be extremely helpful. Clearly evidence of a reaction as drastic as Megan Meier's suicide would not be necessary; indeed the number of cyber bullying cases with so tragic a result should remain mercifully few. But it would be a rare charge of provable electronic bullying that lacked any evidence of harmful consequence – mental or physical illness, time lost from school or work, deterioration of performance, etc. In the application of such a law I would expect courts and juries to be relatively sympathetic and flexible in meeting this condition, so that almost any evidence of effect or impact would suffice. Proof of harmful effect or impact has been crucial in analogous contexts such as criminal neglect, for example.

What seems to me critical, and potentially beneficial, is that in crafting such a law this subcommittee and the Congress demand some such proof of harm, reflecting not only your understanding of the gravity of the offense but also of the need to satisfy First Amendment limitations. I believe you can do both and thus constitutionally target cyber bullies for truly unconscionable speech.

I would be most happy to answer any questions now or to provide information or elaboration to the Subcommittee staff at any time. Thank you for affording me this opportunity to present my views on this vital issue.

Mr. SCOTT. Thank you.
Ms. Warren?

TESTIMONY OF JUDI WESTBERG WARREN, PRESIDENT, WEB WISE KIDS, SANTA ANA, CA

Ms. WARREN. Thank you, Mr. Chairman and Members of the Committee, for inviting me to speak on this very important issue of children's safety.

I represent Web Wise Kids, which is a national nonprofit organization which has reached over 7 million kids within the United States with our programs. We are very thankful that Congress is addressing the issue of the growing need for Internet safety among our youth.

Increasing online safety for children requires a comprehensive solution involving diverse stakeholders, including youth, parents, law enforcement, educators, mental health professionals, industry, and community-based organizations. Web Wise Kids believes strongly that Internet safety education is the most effective way to resolve problems and dangers relating to misuse of the Internet.

In the United States, more than 35 million children in kindergarten through grade 12 have Internet access, and, each year, children are starting to use the Internet at a younger and younger age.

The Internet is a powerful and growing medium, with more than 1 billion Internet users worldwide. The Internet is an invaluable tool, critical to America's ability to compete in a global economy. At the same time, it also poses great challenges to keeping kids safe in a new cyber world.

This dramatic rise in children's use of Internet has led to an increase in risky behaviors, such as cyberstalking and cyberbullying and sexting. Research indicates that youth are at risk online. For example, 43 percent of teens were victims of cyberbullying in 2008, and 33 percent of teenagers have been approached online by a stranger.

Web Wise Kids strongly supports legislation to provide funding for Internet safety programs. New investments in our educational infrastructure will train and equip teachers and law enforcement with the tools they need to teach children to use the Internet and other technologies safely.

Children are integrating technology into their lives at lightning speed. While this is a positive development, State and Federal funding is inadequate to meet that growing need. Students receive little education on safe and ethical Internet use. The majority of responsibility for teaching Internet safety falls on educators, who are often unprepared to provide this type of education.

Federal law mandates that elementary and secondary schools receiving E-rate funding must have an Internet safety education program. However, no funding has been provided to meet this Federal requirement.

Clearly, parents play a significant role. Providing targeted resources to the school system would also effectively help us to reach parents.

Web Wise Kids strongly supports passage of the "AWARE Act" sponsored by Congresswoman Wasserman Schultz and Congressman Culberson, as well as its Senate counterpart sponsored by

Senator Menendez. This legislation is carefully crafted and will provide much-needed funding to support collaborative, comprehensive, and diversified approaches to online safety education in our schools.

The bill's centerpiece is a competitive Internet safety education grant program for State and local education agencies and nonprofit organizations to promote the safe use of digital technologies. The "AWARE Act" identifies clear uses of the funding and includes safeguards to assure an effective research and evaluation component of the program. This legislation will go a long way to protect children and families online.

While administered by the Department of Justice, Web Wise Kids strongly urges the concurrence of the Departments of Education and Health and Human Services in implementing this legislation. Interagency cooperation will allow for sharing insights and information.

We applaud Congresswoman Sánchez for raising awareness of cyberbullying as a significant problem for children in the U.S. Cyberbullying, like offline bullying, can cause substantial harm to our youth, including serious and long-term emotional and behavioral problems. For the victim of cyberbullying, there can be literally no place to run. Prevention of cyberbullying through educating kids on how to respond to online harassment is paramount, in our view.

Imposing punitive sanctions requires careful examination. Targeted criminal penalties against severe forms of harassment might be appropriate if the legislation is able to withstand constitutional scrutiny. The most effective impact Congress can have is providing greater resources to promote Internet safety education in our schools and prevent harm from happening in the first place.

Passage of this legislation, sponsored by Congresswoman Wasserman Schultz and Congressman Culberson, would be a first major step forward. Education builds lessons for a lifetime. With this legislation, we have an opportunity to enhance the skills of educators and provide students with hands-on opportunities to use technology safely and ethically for generations to come.

Thank you.

[The prepared statement of Ms. Warren follows:]

PREPARED STATEMENT OF JUDI WESTBERG WARREN

WEBWISEKIDS
WISDOM BEGINS WITH YOU

Testimony of

Judi Westberg Warren
President
Web Wise Kids
(www.webwisekids.org)

Before the
House Judiciary Committee
Subcommittee on Crime, Terrorism, and Homeland Security

"Cyberbullying and other Online Safety Issues for Children"

September 30, 2009

Mr. Chairman and members of the Subcommittee, thank you for inviting me here today to speak on the important issue of online child safety.

Web Wise Kids is a national non-profit organization dedicated to preventing online child victimization by providing innovative educational tools to educators, parents and children with the aim of helping youth stay safe online. Since 2000, more than 7 million youth and more than one million parents nationwide have been educated by Web Wise Kids' programs on the importance of using the Internet safely and responsibly. We are working successfully with and through state departments of education, regional and local school districts, law enforcement, industry and community-based organizations. Our unique interactive games educate children about Internet safety issues including cyber-bullying, Internet predators, cyber-ethics, safe cell phone use and cyber crime. The games are based on learning theory to maximize retention. They are well evaluated and challenging for the kids. Accompanying resource materials promote meaningful discussions and students have the opportunity to develop their own Internet safety plans.

We applaud increased Congressional awareness of online child safety. Increasing on-line safety for children requires a comprehensive solution involving diverse stakeholders including youth, parents, law enforcement, educators, mental health professionals, industry and community-based organizations.

WEBWISEKIDS
WISDOM BEGINS WITH YOU

Web Wise Kids strongly believes that Internet safety education, coupled with technology tools, is the most effective way to resolve and mitigate problems and dangers relating to misuse of the Internet and other new media. It is vital that we equip individuals and communities with up-to-date information and tools needed to safely, securely, ethically and effectively use the Internet and a variety of other technologies, especially as it relates to the impact of these technologies on our youth.

Use of Internet by Kids Nearly Universal
Use of the Internet by kids is nearly universal. In the United States, more than 35 million children in kindergarten through grade twelve have Internet access. And, each year, children are starting to use the Internet at a younger age.

Today, some 93% of youth ages 12-17 are online and 94% of their parents are online. Nearly 45% of children ages 3 to 11 are projected to use the Internet on a monthly basis this year. 80% of teens 13-17 use cell phones with most mobile devices having built-in cameras. By 2020, the mobile device will be the primary connection to the Internet for most of the world's population, including youth. Use of social media via facebook, twitter, MySpace and other sites is robust among youth: nearly 90% of teens 13-19 have a profile on social media sites. We believe surveys will continue to find greater numbers of children using the Internet at earlier ages.

The Internet is Here to Stay
The Internet is a powerful and growing medium. There are more than 1 billion Internet users worldwide. The Internet provides instant access to research and boundless information and establishes digital connections between individuals around the world. The Internet is an invaluable tool critical to America's ability to compete in a global economy. While the transformation to the digital economy presents a tremendous opportunity for innovation, it also poses great challenges to keeping children safe in a cyber world. There are harmful and significant risks to youth when the Internet is misused.

American Youth are at Risk Online
This dramatic rise in children's use of the Internet has led to an increase in risky behaviors such as cyber-bullying and 'sexting.' Research indicates that youth are at risk online:

- 43% of teens were victims of cyber-bullying in 2008;
- Youth who create Internet content and use social networking sites are more likely to be targets of harmful contact;

- 33% of youth between the ages of 11-16 report exposure to specific type of violent crime on the Internet at least once in the past year;
- 33% of teenagers have been approached online by a stranger;
- 40% of teens said their parents have no idea of their online activities;
- 48% of kindergarten and first graders report viewing online content that made them feel uncomfortable and one-in-four did not report the incident to an adult;
- 21% of 10th-12th graders admit to using a computer or an electronic device to cheat on a school assignment;
- 65% of 10th-12th graders admit to illegally downloading music; and
- 64% of online teens (ages 12-17) stated that they do things online that they don't want their parents to know about, and 79% stated that they aren't careful enough when giving out information about themselves online.

Legislation-Education is Key
For nearly two years, Web Wise Kids has been calling on Congress to pass legislation to substantially increase funding to meet the growing need for Internet safety programs and resources.

New investments in our educational infrastructure are needed for programs and training to equip educators and law enforcement with the tools needed to teach children to safely, securely and ethically use the Internet and a variety of technologies. This investment is critical to providing 21st century tools to educators and law enforcement to prevent online child victimization for millions of children growing up on-line.

We know that children are integrating technology into their lives at lightning speed. While this is a positive trend to prepare a 21st century workforce, state and federal funding is inadequate to meet the growing need and requirements for Internet safety programs. Currently, students receive little education on safe and ethical Internet use. State and local agencies place the majority of responsibility of teaching Internet safety on educators who are unprepared to provide this education.

Federal law now mandates that all schools receiving E-rate funding must have an Internet safety education program but are provided no funding to meet this federal requirement. Specifically, the mandatory Internet safety education must include lessons on cyber bullying awareness and response as well as teaching appropriate online behaviors for students on social networking sites and in chat rooms. Most educators have received little or no professional development on Internet safety. More hands-on training opportunities for educators and increased and on-going education and awareness opportunities for youth throughout the K-12 experience would provide needed investment to help close the gap between danger and knowledge.

Clearly, parents should play a significant role. Just last week, Web Wise Kids participated in a series of meetings and public forums with industry leaders and the Obama Administration where the issue of raising awareness of Internet safety education with parents was identified as a significant need. There are three major challenges in reaching out to parents. First, parents are simply very busy with work and other priorities. Second, children tend to be more advanced users of technology than parents, making it difficult for the parent to have effective conversations about Internet safety. Third, ensuring outreach and awareness efforts actually reach parents with the most effective messages. We know that most parents are connected to their child's school so providing targeted resources to the school system would provide an excellent opportunity effectively reach parents.

Web Wise Kids strongly supports swift enactment of H.R. 3630, the Adolescent Web Awareness Requires Education Act of 2009 (AWARE Act) and its Senate companion sponsored by Senator Menendez, S. 1047. This carefully crafted, bipartisan legislation will provide much needed funding to support collaborative, comprehensive and diversified approaches to online safety education in our schools. The AWARE Act would provide critical resources to America's educational infrastructure to train educators in online risk prevention and empower students and parents with hands-on opportunities to use technology safely for generations to come.

The centerpiece of the legislation is the establishment of a competitive Internet safety education grant program for state and local education agencies and non-profit organizations to promote the safe use of digital technologies. In the ever-changing market of technology and innovation, making this grant program competitive and in partnership with organizations that have expertise in Internet safety is a built-in safeguard against ineffective and outdated approaches.

While not overly-prescriptive, the AWARE Act identifies clear uses of the funding which will go a long way to protect children and families online. The use of funds addresses key areas to improve Internet safety where there is a substantial shortage of resources including:

- developing and implementing Internet safety education programs, including educational technology, multimedia and interactive applications, online resources and lesson plans;
- providing professional training to school teachers and professional staff;

- developing online risk prevention programs for children;
- training and supporting peer-driven Internet safety education initiatives;
- coordinating and funding research initiatives that investigate online risks to children and Internet safety education;
- developing and implementing public education campaigns to promote awareness of online risks to children; and
- educating parents and their children on how to use the Internet safely, responsibly, and ethically and helping parents identify and protect their children from risks relating to use of the Internet.

We also are very pleased that the legislation contains additional safeguards to assure effective implementation of the funds. This bill includes both front-end and ongoing research and evaluation. This research also will include the nature and prevalence of current Internet safety education programs and any evidence-based research conducted on them already. The research will also include findings regarding at-risk children. Research is vital to make sure that the programs identify the serious risks in youth online safety.

While administered by the Department of Justice, Web Wise Kids strongly urges the concurrence of the Departments of Education and Health and Human Services in implementing the legislation. This focused inter-agency cooperation is good public policy and consistent with our long-held view that better understanding the concerns related to youth risk online requires collaboration and sharing insight and information with each other - an essential factor in this fast-changing environment.

As mentioned earlier in our testimony, technology tools also play a very important role in addressing dangers resulting from the misuse of the Internet. Nearly every week, our organization is approached by industry seeking to promote new technologies to help parents and educators deal with unwanted online content or communications.

In his recent testimony before the Federal Communications Commission (FCC)[1], Adam Thierer of The Progress & Freedom Foundation cites research indicating that a majority of parents rely on many alternative methods of controlling online content and Internet use in the home including household media rules. Additionally, Thierer references the staggering diversity of parental control technologies that are available today including filters (network-based and stand-alone); monitoring tools; operating system-level controls; browser tools; walled gardens and child-friendly portals; safe search controls;

[1] September 9, 2009 testimony of Adam D. Thierer, Senior Fellow and Director of the Center for Digital Media Freedom, The Progress & Freedom Foundation, before the Federal Communications Commission

social media safety settings and others. It is for this reason that we are pleased H.R. 3630 and S.1047 are technology neutral – a principle we believe should apply to any legislation dealing with on-line safety.

We have had the opportunity to review legislation, H.R. 1966, sponsored by Congresswoman Linda Sanchez. First, like all Americans, we were heartbroken we when we learned the awful news that Megan Meier had taken her own life. Notwithstanding the subsequent legal decisions, we also were very angry and believe that the actions of Lori Drew were reprehensible.

We applaud the work of Congresswoman Sanchez in raising awareness of cyber bullying as a significant problem for children and schools in the United States. Cyber-bullying, like off-line bullying, can cause substantial harm to our youth, including serious and long-term emotional and behavioral problems. But unlike traditional forms of bullying, cyber-bullying can be more pernicious: hurtful or embarrassing messages can be sent at any time from any place using social media, mobile text messaging, email and other web sites. They can be sent anonymously and distributed more rapidly to wider audiences. For the victim of cyber-bullying, there can be literally nowhere to run - places previously considered safe and private are safe no longer.

Speech that involves harm to others is wrong. Unfortunately, kids throughout history have used hurtful speech against each other. Bullying can cause loneliness, depression, anxiety and low-self esteem. Prevention of cyber bullying and educating kids on how to respond to online harassment is paramount in our view. We are pleased this issue is addressed in both the grant program and research elements in H.R. 3630 and S. 1047.

Nevertheless, the use of additional punitive sanctions requires a careful examination. Web Wise Kids may consider supporting punitive legislation that has targeted criminal sanctions against egregious forms of harassment. One challenge is that many actions that would fall under the definition of cyber bullying are not criminal. Legislation should not criminalize all bullying. It is also important to separate actions of kids versus actions of adults. Any legislation considered must be careful to avoid criminalizing youth-to-youth communications. Moreover, as we have seen with other laws struck down by the courts, legislation imposing punitive sanctions for bullying must be able to withstand constitutional scrutiny. In January of this year, after a ten-year battle, the U.S. Supreme Court rejected the government's latest request to revive the Child Online Protection Act (COPA). The law was struck down as an unconstitutional violation of the First Amendment by lower courts and never went into effect.

WEBWISEKIDS
WISDOM BEGINS WITH YOU

Conclusion

Web Wise Kids supports a comprehensive approach to keeping our children safe online. While youth must understand there are serious consequences to their actions, we must avoid the impulse to use scare tactics and enact legislation based on sensational incidents receiving the most media coverage. Congress can have an immediate and effective impact by providing greater resources to promote Internet safety education in our schools and prevent harm from occurring in the first place.

Education builds lessons for a lifetime. Many educators are not immersed in the new digital reality of students. To keep kids safe online, we have an opportunity to enhance the skills of educators, transform the traditional role of classroom teaching and provide students with hands-on opportunities to use technology safely and ethically for generations to come.

Thank you very much.

Mr. SCOTT. Thank you.
Mr. Silverglate?

TESTIMONY OF HARVEY A. SILVERGLATE, ATTORNEY, ZILKIND, RODRIGUEZ, LUNT & DUNCAN, LLP, CAMBRIDGE, MA

Mr. SILVERGLATE. Thank you for the opportunity to testify this afternoon.

My main occupation is that of a criminal defense and civil liberties trial lawyer, as well as an author. So I have done it, and I have written about it. And I have a certain perspective that I have gained from the enforcement of statutes like this out in the real world.

In 1998, I published the book, "The Shadow University: The Betrayal of Liberty on American Campuses." The book was largely about the enforcement of speech and harassment codes in American campuses of higher education.

In 2009, earlier this year, I published another book, called "Three Felonies a Day: How the Feds Target the Innocent." I am leaving a copy of each book here when I leave. You can use it as you wish, or not.

But the impetus to publish these two books grew out of my observations in some of the cases that I tried. There are two problems that I noticed, both of which are present in this bill, the "Cyberbullying Prevention Act."

First of all, there is a problem with the vagueness in the definition of the criminal conduct. And vagueness, incidentally, is distinct from overcriminalization. I have problems with overcriminalizing too many things, but at least if the statute is clear, you know where the lines are drawn. This statute has a significant vagueness problem, and that vagueness problem is exacerbated by the fact that it impinges on protected speech.

I beg to differ with Professor O'Neil, but if one looks at the Supreme Court's decision in *Hustler Magazine v. Falwell,* that was a case where the court, 8 to 0, unanimously overturned a verdict for Reverend Falwell against Hustler Magazine for the intentional infliction of emotional distress. The constitutional issue here is hardly clear. You don't usually get eight-to-nothing opinions of the Supreme Court, where there is no constitutional problem.

But my experience with harassment codes on college campuses tells me that this statute is going to cause a lot of problems, not only legal, but also it is going to prevent a lot of speech which is and should be constitutionally protected.

I actually, after publishing "The Shadow University," I had to start a nonprofit foundation called the Foundation for Individual Rights in Education in order to help the hundreds and hundreds—in fact, it is more than hundreds, it is thousands—of students who were, themselves, harassed by their colleges because they deigned to say things which were deemed by somebody else to be harassing or exceedingly unpleasant.

Now, in "Three Felonies a Day," I have catalogued scores of cases in the criminal justice arena where this same problem arises, people who are convicted for doing things that a lot of us would look at and say, well, wait a minute, how could that be a crime? And the cyberbullying bill uses the same kinds of terms that have caused such problems on campuses: "intimidate," "harass," "cause substantial emotional distress." These are terms that ordinary people, intelligent people, would differ as to what falls within one or another category.

Essentially, this bill would criminalize communications that are very unpleasant, very annoying to the recipients. It will doubtless result in the charging of a substantial number of people whose activities are protected or should be by the first amendment. And, by its mere existence on the statute books, it will deter a vast number of people from exercising speech in a vast number of circumstances where we would all agree it should be protected.

I am not making a case here for harassment. I don't consider it our friend. True harassment is already covered more than adequately by State and even by Federal law via statutes outlawing and punishing true threats and other extreme conduct.

All this bill would do, in my view, is criminalize existing tort law and federalize a perfectly adequate array of State statutes that criminalize true threats that are well understood within the common law tradition. So this bill would really, I fear, confuse citizens while deterring a vast array of constitutionally protected speech.

Thank you.

[The prepared statement of Mr. Silverglate follows:]

PREPARED STATEMENT OF HARVEY A. SILVERGLATE

Congress of the United States
House of Representatives
Committee on the Judiciary
Subcommittee on Crime, Terrorism, and Homeland Security
Hon. Bobby Scott, Chairman

Testimony of

Harvey A. Silverglate
Criminal defense and civil liberties trial lawyer
Author
Adjunct Scholar, Cato Institute

Concerning

The Megan Meier Cyberbullying Prevention Act (H.R. 1966);
The Adolescent Web Awareness Requires Education Act (H.R. 3630)

September 30, 2009

Harvey A. Silverglate
Attorney-at-law & Writer
607 Franklin Street
Cambridge, MA 02139
www.harveysilverglate.com
has@harveysilverglate.com

I am pleased to have been asked to testify on H.R. 1966 (the "Megan Meier Cyberbullying Prevention Act") on behalf of the Cato Institute, where I serve as an Adjunct Scholar.

I approach the problem presented by this legislation not from the vantage point of a legal scholar, however. The Subcommittee, I'm certain, has ample access to members of the professoriate as well as to scholars at the various think tanks with which the Nation in general and Washington in particular are blessed. Indeed, I appear today on behalf of the libertarian Cato Institute, which over the years has presented cogent scholarly studies of many pieces of legislation that have posed threats to American liberty. But I believe that Cato has asked me to appear, and the Subcommittee has invited my testimony, because I have considerable real-world experience as a criminal defense and civil liberties trial lawyer and author who – having never served in government office – has a particular view of the role that certain types of federal legislation play in the day-to-day life of the Republic and in the lives of its citizens.

I have seen, in particular, the ways in which unwise legislation – legislation often born of good intentions – has adversely affected individuals investigated for or accused of federal crimes. Many of these individuals, including (but hardly limited to) clients of mine, have wondered how they could have been investigated, prosecuted, convicted and even sentenced to prison for engaging in conduct that a reasonable person would not have believed to lie within the ambit of the criminal law. Sometimes such a person's actions are within the range of entirely civil and proper, while at other times they approach the edges of the socially acceptable. But unless one's conduct is clearly over the legal line, shock is a perfectly understandable reaction to a criminal charge.

This Subcommittee, as well as other subcommittees and committees of the Congress, has heard much testimony in recent years objecting to proposed legislation on grounds of federalism – the notion that the federal government has been unduly encroaching on areas of life and commerce that in theory were supposed to have been regulated by the states. One could pose a cogent critique of the proposed "Cyberbullying" legislation on such grounds, in my view, but this is not my purpose today. One could also point out, as other scholars and organizations have, that criminal legislation has been imposed on areas of American life that should not be subject to criminal law and criminal sanctions – a phenomenon known as "overcriminalization" – and that this law would represent one further step in that dangerous direction. But arguing overcriminalization is not my purpose today.

Rather, I wish to focus on another, often overlooked aspect of the proposed "Cyberbullying" legislation, growing out of its *vagueness*.

My assessment and criticism of the bill lie primarily in the area of due process of law enshrined in the Fifth Amendment, with consequent repercussions for First Amendment free speech rights. I believe that this law would not be comprehensible to the average citizen – and, indeed, to the average lawyer or judge for that matter. It does not help understanding, of course, when vague terms such as "intimidate, harass, or cause substantial emotional distress" are used in a *criminal* statute to define *verbal* conduct that can land one in federal prison. A typical citizen cannot be expected to understand how and where to draw a line, not only because of the inherent vagueness of the terms, but also because in this instance the prohibited conduct involves solely speech – and speech, citizens are taught to believe from kindergarten on, is (or at least is supposed to be) free in America.

Hence, it is the combination of Fifth Amendment due process notions and First Amendment free speech doctrine that makes this proposed legislation particularly lethal to liberty interests. This presents us all – legislators and citizens, laymen and lawyers, political activists, scholars, and everyone who speaks his or her mind virtually every day in this often fractious (but thankfully free) nation of ours – with a profound challenge: How can we protect legitimate societal interests without posing traps for the unwary innocent?

My perspective on this, as I've said, is a product of four decades of experience as a criminal defense and civil liberties trial lawyer, as well as a civil liberties activist and a frequent writer on these phenomena. In these capacities, I have dealt directly with the socially unhealthy curtailments of free speech and of due process by the uses – and misuses – of various kinds of regulations aimed at curtailing "harassment," "hostile behavior," and other such vague terms around which this legislation is built. (In the context of this legislation, it is likely that the term "behavior" is referring primarily, if not exclusively, to speech.) Often born of good intentions, these legislative efforts have, almost without fail, produced unintended consequences, including excessive and unfair prosecutions as well as the inhibition of the sometimes unruly verbal interactions that are, and should be, the product of a free society.

As one can see from my *curriculum vitae* that I am submitting separately to the Subcommittee, a significant portion of my legal career has been devoted to defending academic freedom on American college and university campuses. I have litigated and advocated extensively on behalf of college and university students and faculty members in campus administrative tribunals – people who have been charged with and often disciplined for violations of campus "harassment" codes. In many of those cases, the "harassment" has been nothing more than expression of speech clearly, or at least arguably, protected by free speech and academic freedom standards. (In public universities, of course, First Amendment protections directly apply, while students and teachers at private institutions must rely on those institutions' voluntary adherence to traditional principles and protections of academic freedom.) I wrote about this problem – the serious threat to academic freedom as well as to the well-being of students who are trying to get through college without unfair blemish to their records and reputations – in my co-authored 1998 book, *The Shadow University: The Betrayal of Liberty on America's Campuses* (Free Press, 1998; paperback currently in print from HarperPerennial), a copy of which I am providing to the Subcommittee. (An appended excerpt demonstrates the intractable problems encountered in trying to enforce, in the context of the campus equivalent of a criminal proceeding, a code that employs such terms as "harassment" in order to penalize speech.)[1]

Indeed, a 1992 incident at my *alma mater*, the Harvard Law School, demonstrates in very stark terms the problematic results of punishing, or even merely threatening to punish, harsh but constitutionally-protected expression. After the tragic murder of Professor Mary Joe Frug, a feminist legal scholar at the New England School of Law, the *Harvard Law Review* published one of her unfinished articles, a spirited and sometimes offensive critique of law and mores from a radical feminist perspective. In response, a group of students on the *Law Review* staff wrote a biting parody of the article – a critique not only of the ideas presented in the piece, but also of the decision by the august *Harvard Law Review* to run a piece of unfinished scholarship for what some deemed unacceptably politically correct reasons. An outcry against the student parodists ensued. A group of Harvard Law School professors belonging to the school's disciplinary committee – known as the Administrative Board – concluded that such "verbal harassment" could be penalized only if there were a regulation or code prohibiting such speech.

The Harvard Law faculty, in a moment when emotion clearly overcame loyalty to academic freedom and free speech principles, promptly adopted such a speech code, dubbed a "sexual harassment" code. Harvard Law School now has the equivalent of its own "bullying" statute, and the state of parody and discourse at the school is much the poorer. Indeed, the annual April Fools' Day publication of the satiric *Harvard Law Revue*, which contained the aforesaid parody of the feminist legal scholar's article, ceased publication shortly thereafter.[2] Parody and satire are, of course, very important tools of critical thought and political and social expression in our society generally, and in academia in particular. Aside from the untoward social, political and intellectual consequences of discouraging the free exchange of ideas by means of a code so vague that students speak out on "hot button" topics at their own considerable risk, one needs to consider the unfairness of threatening to ruin a student's educational record because he or she operated on the misunderstanding that America is a free country and that campuses, in particular, value uninhibited and robust speech.

Such is the free speech mischief encountered by an academic institution's attempt to outlaw, under the rubric of "harassment," all manner and kind of unpleasant, acerbic, unsettling speech. The problem has arisen at many other campuses, and the judicial response, when litigation has been initiated by students, has been unambiguous: several federal district courts and courts of appeals have rejected the use of such vague terms as "harassment" in the context of restrictions on unpleasant campus speech.[3]

Consider, for example, an incident in 2008 at Indiana University – Purdue University Indianapolis (IUPUI). A university employee/student was found guilty of racial harassment for reading a book titled *Notre Dame vs. the Klan: How the Fighting Irish Defeated the Ku Klux Klan*. In a letter announcing and justifying the charges, the IUPUI administration explained that the student "used extremely poor judgment by insisting on openly reading the book related to a historically and racially abhorrent subject in the presence of your Black coworkers."[4] Facing public pressure, and recognizing the questionable legal grounds on which the decision stood, IUPUI dropped the harassment charges in May 2008. This episode exemplified how a campus "harassment" code can be stretched to cover activity as innocuous as reading literature on a controversial subject.

To be sure, there are differences between a university setting (where freedom of inquiry and of expression are of the utmost importance) on the one hand, and that of society at large (where *reasonable* restrictions are more tolerable). Nonetheless, my experience with suppression of speech on campuses, and the case law striking down these harassment codes, are pertinent to this bill. Whether on a campus quad or in a public park, the same line of reasoning applies: In a free society, people will be offended, feelings will be hurt. Yet separating unsavory speech – even quite clearly disagreeable and offensive speech – from *criminal* conduct is absolutely imperative in a democratic system that celebrates freedom of expression.

The Supreme Court of the United States, in a unanimous decision in the 1988 case of *Hustler Magazine, Inc. vs. Falwell*, 485 U.S. 46, reaffirmed that even painful parody is constitutionally protected by the First Amendment. In that landmark case, *Hustler* publisher Larry Flynt used a fake Compari liquor ad to suggest that his ideological adversary, Reverend Jerry Falwell, had lost his virginity in a drunken encounter with his own mother in an outhouse. The point made by the justices was, and remains, that the First Amendment must protect even very offensive and unsettling speech. "From the viewpoint of history it is clear that our political discourse would have been considerably poorer without" such depictions, concluded Chief Justice William Rehnquist. This was in a *civil* litigation context where a defamation plaintiff was claiming that he was the victim of Flynt's magazine article that constituted "the intentional infliction of emotional distress." A unanimous Supreme Court, recognizing that indeed painful distress was inflicted, nevertheless reversed a *civil* money judgment against the publisher. It is perfectly obvious that a *criminal* charge would have fared even more poorly under constitutional scrutiny.

The Subcommittee is now considering a bill that would *criminally* penalize painful language that seeks to inflict distress. The bill would apply only to speech, rather than to the myriad physical actions that typically accompany a harassment claim in, for example, the workplace. Hence, not only would enactment of this statute provoke a veritable storm of constitutional litigation, but it would, even in the absence of litigation, create a chill over a vast expanse of unpleasant but protected speech. And, it bears repeating, the definitions used are exceedingly vague.

Current law, both state and federal, bans a considerable array of speech that society, state and federal legislatures, and the courts agree constitutes either a criminal threat (*e.g.*, extortion) or a genuine tort. Furthermore, the law governing free speech has for a very long time outlawed, in either a criminal or civil arena, speech that might otherwise be protected but that transgresses acceptable *time, place* and *manner* requirements. For example, it would be constitutionally protected to drive up and down a street at 3 o'clock in the afternoon (appropriate *time*), with a loudspeaker (effective *manner*, given the need to have one's political message heard), in the Downtown part of a city (appropriate *place* for public campaigning) touting one's preferred candidate for political office. The same message would be considered a tort or even (in an extreme case) a crime (such as "disturbing the peace") if one were to deliver it via loudspeaker in a *residential* neighborhood at 3 o'clock in the *morning*.

Those prepared to enact this bill must ask themselves whether the protection of speech (in particular) from undue curtailment is somehow invalidated simply because the *means* employed to transmit unwelcome messages happen to be electronic. In other words, if this bill were drafted with identical language, but "electronic means" were replaced by "printed means," would the constitutional conflicts be any more, or less, apparent? Such a bill would expose the ranks of newspaper reporters, for example, to criminal prosecution for causing "substantial emotional distress" in fulfilling their democratic watchdog responsibilities. An exposé of corrupt (or even some ordinary) political activity surely causes "emotional distress" to its subject. Should these same words, when transmitted via electronic means, cause their author to fear the wrath of federal criminal law? It is vastly important, as our society becomes increasingly technologically oriented, that protections of our fundamental freedoms be applied to new modes of communication as well as to the traditional modalities.

One may claim that curtailing political expression is not the intent of this legislation; instead, it is meant to stop "cyber bullies" from causing distress to minors. Nowhere in the language of this proposed legislation, however, can any such assurance be found. To have Congress jump into the fray surrounding the control of offensive messages sent over electronic media – especially by means of a legislative vehicle which uses a vague concept like "hostile behavior" and "harassment" that causes "substantial emotional distress" – would be more of a trap for the unwary than a useful social tool. Not only is the proposed "Cyberbullying" statute vague by its own terms, but the array of speech that it would discourage surely is vast, since people tend to severely limit their speech when they even think that they *might* otherwise roam into prohibited territory. Thus, *vague* statutes also function, invariably, as *overbroad* prohibitions in that in practice they prevent an array of speech far broader than the presumed statutory target.

My current book, *Three Felonies a Day: How the Feds Target the Innocent* (Encounter Books, September 2009), deals with a wide variety of injustices caused by unacceptably vague federal criminal statutes. (I am submitting a copy of the book along with this presentation and my testimony.) This book is written from the perspective of a trial lawyer who has seen these statutes wreak havoc with the law and with people's lives, and threaten the balance between governmental authority and civil society. The book contains some legal analysis, but primarily it is meant as a description of how vague statutes function, in practice, as a tool of terror and true prosecutorial harassment in the lives of ordinary as well as extraordinary people.

In my book, there are many examples of the mischief caused by vague criminal statutes in all areas of civil society. One chapter examines how the federal anti-corruption laws, on account of vagueness, are used to unfairly harass and prosecute governmental officials, state as well as federal. I have appended to this written submission an excerpt from the text that seeks to explain the nature and scope of the problem posed by vague criminal statutes.[5]

There is, in my view, currently a veritable epidemic caused by the proliferation of prosecutions based upon vague federal statutes. I was readily able, from my own litigation experience as well as from research done on other cases, to pinpoint myriad inappropriate prosecutions of many an unwary innocent citizen in the medical community, the medical device and pharmaceutical manufacturing industry, investment houses, bankers, lawyers, accountants and auditors, academics, artists, newspaper reporters, merchants, as well as public officials. The time has come, it seems to me, to *reduce or eliminate* – rather than to enlarge – the number of these affronts to liberty and fair treatment of our citizens. It is difficult enough for a law-abiding citizen to keep track of all of his or her *clear* legal obligations. We citizens should not be faced with an ever-growing number of vague statutes that threaten liberty by failing to define precisely what conduct might constitute yet another new felony.

I selected the title of my book – *Three Felonies a Day* – from a notion that occurred to me when I was defending one after another client whose conduct was, in my view, particularly innocuous, and who faced serious felony charges nonetheless. My thought was that a typical professional gets up in the morning, has breakfast, sends the children off to school, goes to work, spends the day dealing with matters that entail the use of the mails or other facilities of interstate communication or commerce, comes home, has dinner, puts the kids to sleep, finishes the day's newspapers, and goes to sleep. Little does such a citizen know that he or she has likely committed three arguable federal felonies that day – a problem that would ripen into a life-unsettling event only if somehow he or she were to come within the sights of a federal prosecutor. Congress should be seeking to lessen this problem, not add to it. In my view, the "Cyberbullying" bill creates more problems than it could possibly solve, especially in view of the fact that existing law is already more than adequate to deal with truly outrageous or dangerous harassment.

---

[1] Appendix 1.
[2] I have written about this controversy, available at http://thephoenix.com/Boston/News/65590-Parody-flunks-out/, and have appended to this submission a copy of my article. (Appendix 2.)
[3] In April 2009, the *Harvard Law Review* criticized a decision from the U.S. Court of Appeals for the Third Circuit in which the court struck down a harassment code at Temple University (*DeJohn v. Temple University*, 537 F.3d 301 (3d Cir. 2008)). Kelly Sarabyn, former Jackson fellow at FIRE, wrote on *the Torch* (FIRE's blog: http://www.thefire.org/torch/) that this *HLR* comment disregarded a string of federal court decisions that struck down campus harassment codes. Sarabyn listed the cases and citations:

> *Dambrot v. Central Michigan University*, 55 F.3d 1177 (6th Cir. 1995) (declaring university discriminatory harassment policy facially unconstitutional); *College Republicans at San Francisco State University v. Reed*, 523 F. Supp. 2d 1005 (N.D. Cal. 2007) (enjoining enforcement of university civility policy); *Roberts v. Haragan*, 346 F. Supp. 2d 853 (N.D. Tex. 2004) (finding university sexual harassment policy unconstitutionally overbroad); *Bair v. Shippensburg University*, 280 F. Supp. 2d 357 (M.D. Pa. 2003) (enjoining enforcement of university harassment policy due to overbreadth); *Booher v. Board of Regents*, 1998 U.S. Dist. LEXIS 11404 (E.D. Ky. Jul. 21, 1998) (finding university sexual harassment policy void for vagueness and overbreadth); *The UWM Post, Inc. v. Board of Regents of the University of Wisconsin System*, 774 F. Supp. 1163 (E.D. Wis. 1991) (declaring university racial and discriminatory harassment policy facially unconstitutional); *Doe v. University of Michigan*, 721 F. Supp. 852 (E.D. Mich. 1989) (enjoining enforcement of university discriminatory harassment policy due to unconstitutionality).

[4] A video produced by the Foundation for Individual Rights in Education (FIRE), a nonprofit organization of which I am the Chairman and co-founder, can be accessed at: http://www.thefire.org/article/10067.html.
[5] Appendix 3.

APPENDIX 1

THE SHADOW UNIVERSITY
*The Betrayal of Liberty on America's Campuses**

By Alan C. Kors and Harvey A. Silverglate

"SHUT UP," THEY REASONED: SILENCING STUDENTS

A tour of the nation's campuses is not encouraging for friends of student rights. Almost *all* colleges and universities, for example, have "verbal behavior" provisions in their codes, and *most* of the cases in this book involve assaults at various levels on student speech. If this chapter were a visit to every landmark of censorship, it would become a numbing encyclopedia of repression. Let us look at some snapshots of America's campuses, then to understand the landscape. These policies and practices can change, year by year—for better or for worse—but this is what occurred in the shadow universities of the 1980s and 1990s.

New England

Sometimes, policies say it all. In New England, "harassment" has included, within recent times, jokes and way of telling stories "experienced by others as harassing" (Bowdoin College); "verbal behavior" that produces "feelings of impotence," "anger," or "disenfranchisement," whether "intentional or unintentional" (Brown University); speech that CAUSES LOSS OF "self-esteem [or] a vague sense of danger" (Colby College); or even "inappropriately directed laughter," inconsiderate jokes," and "stereotyping"

---

* This passage is excerpted from Alan Charles Kors and Harvey A. Silverglate, *The Shadow University: The Betrayal of Liberty on America's Campuses* (New York: The Free Press, 1998; New York: HarperPerennial, 1999).

(University of Connecticut). The student code of the University of Vermont demands that its students not only not offend each other, but that they appreciate each other: "Each of us must assume responsibility for becoming educated about racism, sexism, ageism, homophobia/heterosexism, and other forms of oppression so that we may respond to other community members in an understanding and appreciative manner." Its very "Freedom of Expression and Dissent Policy" warns: "Nothing in these regulations shall be construed as authorizing or condoning unpermitted and unprotected speech, such as fighting words."[1]

Sometimes, however, policies tell us nothing. In 1975, Yale University rejected the call for speech codes and adopted a policy of full protection for free expression. Yale embraced "unfettered freedom, the right to think the unthinkable, discuss the unmentionable, and challenge the unchallengeable," and it explicitly rejected the notion that "solidarity," "harmony," "civility," or "mutual respect" could be higher values than "free expression" at a university. Even when individuals "fail to meet their social and ethical responsibilities," Yale guaranteed, "the paramount obligation of the university is to protect their right to free expression."[2]

In 1986, however, Yale sophomore Wayne Dick—a Christian conservative—distributed a handout satirizing Yale's GLAD, Gay and Lesbian Awareness Days. It announced the celebration of "BAD, Bestiality Awareness Days," and listed such lectures as "PAN: the Goat, the God, the Lover" and a discussion of "Rover v. Wade." On May 2, Patricia Pearce, the associate dean of Yale College, informed Dick by letter that both an administrative member of the dean's office's Racial and Ethnic Harassment Board and a gay activist had "submitted…a complaint alleging harassment in t he form of a "BAD week 86' poster." The college's Executive Committee Coordinating Group had decided that the charge that Dick's poster violated a ban on "physical restriction, assault, coercion, or intimidation" had merit, and that it should be submitted to the full committee. According to Dick, as reported in the *Village Voice* in July 1986, when he asked Dean Pearce how this satiric flier could be actionable if Yale's policy guaranteed full freedom of expression and the right to "challenge the unchallengeable," she replied that it did not protect "worthless speech." On May 13, the Executive Committee found Dick guilty of harassment and intimidation.[3] His mother told the *Boston Globe*: "Wayne…feels very strongly about things. He expresses himself freely." At Yale, that earned him two years of probation.[4]

A code, absent a commitment to freedom, will mean whatever power wants it to mean. Assisting a student at Wesleyan University against violations of the speech code in the spring of 1996, Robert Chatelle, of the National Writers Union, wrote to Wesleyan's president and quoted from the university's official policy: "'Harassment Harassment and abuse…may include…verbal harassment and abuse.' You don't need a Ph.D. in logic to notice that…verbal harassment is *anything* [Wesleyan] decides it to be."[5] Dartmouth College even decided that free expression was, literally, garbage. In 1993, some students repeatedly stole the conservative *Dartmouth Review* from dormitory delivery sites. The dean of students announced that the confiscations did not violate the code of student conduct. As an official Dartmouth spokesman explained *The Dartmouth Review* was "litter."[6]

In Fall 1995, Emerson College barred the college's student radio station from playing "rap music" not on a list of forty officially approved pieces that contained no "trigger words." The administration insisted that rap was sexist and caused crime. Arthur Barron, chairman of the Department of Mass Communication, explained: "We want to make absolutely certain that nothing in the body of rap music inspires, incites, either violence or sexism or hatred."[7] James D'Entremont, director of the Boston Coalition for Freedom of Expression, wrote to Barron: "No amount of brain-dead social engineering through censorship is ever going to give us a safer campus or a kinder and gentler society."[8]

Tufts University, in academic year 1988-89, placed a student on disciplinary probation (and sentenced him to fifty hours of community service, later rescinded) for having sold T-shirts with the motto "Why Beer is Better Than Women at Tufts." It listed such reasons as "Beer Never Has a Headache," "You Can Share a Beer With Your Friends," and "If You Pour a Beer Right, You'll Always Get Good Head." These statements, Tufts ruled, created an "offensive" and "sexist" environment. If selling the T-shirt violated the speech provisions of Tufts's harassment policy, however, wearing the T-Shirt also did, which created a problem for the administration, because the T-shirt had sold well. President Jean Mayer divided the campus into "free-speech" and "non-free-speech" zones. The speech provisions did not apply to the privacy of one's own room or to campus lawns, but they governed dormitory common areas and classrooms.[9]

Most universities have accepted speech codes passively, but students at Tufts, after seven months of debate and public forums about freedom of expression, formed a broad nonpartisan coalition in defense of their rights. Tufts students marked off the physical boundaries between "free" and "un-free" zones with tape and chalk, and they invited the media in. The campus looked like Berlin in 1946. Embarrassed, President

Mayer rescinded the speech code.[10] Tufts's next president, John DiBaggio, in a 1996 op-ed in the *Boston Globe*, wrote that "countering hate speech [and] disciplining the hater…[are] worth every effort" in principle, but, alas, "editorial writers and lawyers…with an easy-to-construct argument—namely, 'Free Speech is good'—don't understand that," which invariably lets "the bigots against whom the speech codes are directed merely dance on the college quad." Speech codes, he concluded, have brought "ridicule on places where great ideas are born." Also, "one day those codes may be turned against their authors."[11] There are more principled defenses of free speech (and the belief that "Free Speech is good" was not, to say the least, "easy to construct"), but this will do.

Authors of these codes rarely make their full agenda explicit, but sometimes a document sheds real light. In June 1989, the Massachusetts Board of Regents adopted a statewide "Policy Against Racism" for higher education. It "proscribes all conditions and all actions or omissions including all acts of verbal harassment or abuse which deny or have the effects of denying to anyone his or her rights to equality, dignity, and security on the basis of his or her race, color, ethnicity, culture or religion." It mandated both "appreciation for cultural/racial pluralism" and "a unity and cohesion in the diversity which we seek to achieve," outlawing "racism in any form, expressed or implied, intentional, or inadvertent, individual or institutional." The regents pledged "to eradicate racism, ethnic and cultural offenses and religious intolerance," and "required," among other things, programs "to enlighten faculty, administrators, staff, and students with regard to…ways in which the dominant society manifests and perpetuates racism."[12]

They did not call for any program on political tolerance. At the state's flagship campus, the University of Massachusetts-Amherst, in the spring and summer of 1992, the student newspaper, the *Collegian*, lost all real protection of the rule of law.[13] At an angry rally on the campus after the acquittal of the Los Angeles police officers in the Rodney King affair, protestors turned their hatred against the supposed "racism" of the *Collegian*, which had referred to the L.A. "riots," unlike Professor John Bracey, later head of the Faculty Senate, who at the rally termed the rioters "our warriors." Protestors invaded the offices of the *Collegian*, smashing windows, destroying property, and assaulting with a baseball bat and dragging him to the Student Center (the municipal court sentenced him to counseling). The *Collegian* appealed to the university for protection, but was refused. Editors and staff did get a police escort to another municipality, and published a few editions in hiding, but these were stolen and destroyed. Marc Elliott, editor-in-chief, told the *Boston Globe* that it was "like a Nazi book burning."[14]Undefended by the university, the editors of the *Collegian* surrendered, and they accepted an editorial structure of separate editors and sections for every "historically oppressed" minority on campus. Managing editor Daniel Wetzel told the *Daily Hampshire Gazette*, "There's 100 people running scared right now, and 100 people intimidating them…I'm not going to put a student organization above my safety."[15] He told the Associated Press, "We gave up our journalistic integrity for the safety of the students."[16]

When the *Collegian* appealed for protection, UMass's chancellor Richard O'Brien, replied that there was a conflict between two values that "the university holds dear: protection of free expression and the creation of a multicultural community free of harassment and intimidation." Publicly, he proclaimed neutrality and offered help in solving the "dispute."[17] Privately, according to Marc Elliott, "We were told by the administration that the choice was to give in or let the campus break up in a race riot where people would get killed." Chancellor O'Brien denied that, and told the press, "We were there to facilitate discussion, not to take any side on the issue."[18]

In 1994, in response to an inquiry about the actions taken by the administration in 1992, the new chancellor David K. Scott, replied, in writing: "*Collegian* takeover of May 1, 1992: charges were not brought; Whitmore occupation of May 1, 1992: no disciplinary action was taken; Theft of copies of *Collegian* May 4, 1992: individuals who may have taken copies of the *Collegian* were never identified. It is difficult to call the action theft because the paper is distributed to the public free of charge." As for the physical assault and the destruction of the newspapers: "I am not aware of any specific statements by the administration in response to the incident with the *Collegian* photographer or the theft of copies of the *Collegian*."[19]

In 1995, Chancellor Scott proposed a new harassment policy that would outlaw not only "epithets" and "slurs," but, in addition, "negative stereotyping."[20] The policy caught the eye of the media. *New York Time* columnist Anthony Lewis illustrated the gulf between liberal and campus views of freedom. UMass's policy, he wrote, would "create a totalitarian atmosphere in which everyone would have to guard his tongue all the time lest he say something that someone finds offensive." Lewis asked: "Do the drafters have no knowledge of history?...No understanding that freedom requires…'freedom for the thought that we hate'? And if not, what are they doing at a university?" He concluded that the elastic concept of a "'hostile environment'" intolerably menaced "freedom of speech, at universities of all places."[21]

Tell that to Harvard Law School, which in October 1995 adopted, by an overwhelming vote of its faculty, "Sexual Harassment Guidelines" that ban "speech…of a sexual nature that is unwelcome,…abusive…and has the…effect of…creating an intimidating, demeaning, degrading, hostile or otherwise seriously offensive…educational environment."[22] Harvard, though a private institution, prides itself on being a citadel of legal education on liberty, but it adopted these rules years after federal district courts had ruled that similar codes violated the First Amendment.[23] Indeed, the guidelines seem to have been enacted precisely in order to suppress speech on the heels of a great campus controversy involving a law student parody of an expletive-filled *Harvard Law Review* article, "A Postmodern Feminist Legal Manifesto," published as a posthumous gesture toward Mary Jo Frug, a radical feminist legal scholar (and the wife of a member of Harvard Law School's faculty) who had been brutally murdered some months earlier.[24] When the parodists bitingly mocked the decision to publish, there were calls from some outraged students and faculty for their discipline or even expulsion. Professor David Kennedy brought formal charges against the students before Harvard Law School's disciplinary body, but those charges were dismissed—not on the basis of academic freedom, but because there was no code of conduct at the law school that would have forbidden the students' words.[25] A year later, the faculty adopted the guidelines that almost certainly would have supplied a basis for punishment of the authors of what was clearly a political parody.

[1] All policies on "harassment" and "verbal behavior" have been taken from the Webpages and handbooks of the colleges and universities discussed during the period 1994-97, unless otherwise indicated.

[2] Yale University, "Report of the Committee on Freedom of Expression at Yale" (the "Woodward Committee" report), January 1975; Yale University, "Free Expression, Peaceful Dissent, and Demonstrations," in Yale's published policies and procedures, still in force.

[3] For the details of the Wayne Dick case, see Nat Hentoff, "An Unspeakable Crime at Yale," *Village Voice*, July 15, 1986; Nat Hentoff, "The Trial of a Notorious Yale Student," *Village Voice*, July 22, 1986; and John Hechinger, "Civil Liberties, Battle Lines Set at Yale. Student's Antigay Poster Raises Free Speech Issue," *Boston Globe*, July 29, 1986.

[4] *Boston Globe*, July 29, 1986.

[5] Copy of letter in possession of authors.

[6] *Columbia Journalism Review*, October 1994.

[7] *Boston Phoenix*, October 27, 1995; *Boston Herald*, November 1, 1995; *The ROC: the Voice of Rock Out Censorship*, December 1995/January 1996.

[8] Copy of letter in possession of authors.

[9] On the details of the T-shirt and speech code episode at Tufts, see Tufts University, "Freedom of Speech Versus Freedom From Harassment," a policy adopted in spring 1989 and published by the university in "Policies and Responsibilities," 1989-1990; *Tufts Daily*, "Commencement Issue" (May 21, 1989), and all issues throughout September and October 1989; *Boston Phoenix*, October 13, 1989.

[10] *Tufts Daily*, September, October 1989, passim.

[11] *Boston Globe*, March 17, 1996.

[12] Commonwealth of Massachusetts Board of Regents of Higher Education, "Policy Against Racism. Guidelines for Campus Policies Against Racism," adopted June 13, 1989. A copy of these guidelines, which were distributed to high administrators, is in possession of the authors.

[13] On the turmoil surrounding the newspaper takeover, see Gary Crosby Brasor, "Turmoil and Tension at the University of Massachusetts at Amherst: History, Analysis, Recommended Solutions," a seventy-nine-page report issued by the Massachusetts Association of Scholars in November 1994, and the report's fifty-three-page "Update," issued in March 1996. See also, Massachusetts Advisory Committee to the U.S. Commission on Civil Rights, "Campus Tensions in Massachusetts: Searching for Solutions in the Nineties," October 1992.

[14] *Boston Globe*, May 7, 1992.

[15] *Daily Hampshire Gazette*, May 7, 1992.

[16] Associated Press, May 7, 1992.

[17] *Boston Globe*, May 7, 1992.

[18] *Daily Hampshire Gazette*, May 9, 1992.

[19] Letter from Chancellor David K. Scott to Gray Brasor, April 7, 1994 (copy in possession of authors).

[20] Office of the Chancellor, University of Massachusetts, "Letter from Chancellor Scott to campus community," October 11, 1995, sent with letter from Susan Pearson, Associate Chancellor, September 20, 1995, with attached "Proposed Harassment Policy."

[21] *New York Times*, November 27, 1995.

[22] Memorandum from Harvard Law School dean Robert C. Clark announcing the enforcement of HLS sexual harassment guideline, October 25, 1995.

[23] *UWM Post v. Board of Regents of the University of Wisconsin*, 774 F.Supp. 1163 (E.D. Wis. 1991); *Doe v. University of Michigan*, 721 F.Supp. 852 (E.D. Mich. 1989).

[24] See Mary Jo Frug, "A Postmodern Feminist Legal Manifesto," 105 *Harvard Law Review* (1992) 1045 and parody, "He-Manifesto of Post-Mortem Legal Feminism," 105 *Harvard Law Revue* (1992), pp. 61-62.

[25] The Harvard Law School Administrative Board's ruling is dated May 21, 1992, and is in the possession of the authors, along with other papers and reports concerning Professor Kennedy's efforts to discipline the parodists.

APPENDIX 2

THE PHOENIX

Parody Flunks Out

Political humor is no longer welcome in Academia as administrators choke the life out of parody

FREEDOM WATCH | Harvey Silverglate | 7/30/2008

When I first saw the cover — yes, *that* cover — of the *New Yorker*, I expected the swift and nauseatingly self-righteous condemnation it received from the TV personalities and politically correct pundits. That's par for the course in the knee-jerk, brain-dead, humor-free Oughts. But what caught me off guard, even in this Age of Cynicism, was that Barack Obama joined their ranks: his official campaign spokesman, Bill Burton, labeled the lampoon "tasteless and offensive."

Artist Barry Blitt's brilliant illustration — which sought to satirize the naysayers who portray Obama as a flag-burning, unpatriotic Muslim and his wife as a black-power radical — cut to the core of today's political paradox. The cover received so much attention, it has even led to meta-parodies, the most amusing of which was offered by the *New Yorker's* sister publication *Vanity Fair*, which depicted a wobbly, walker-wielding John McCain and his wife in the same setting and artistic style. Still, the Illinois senator's heated, visceral attack of the parody led me to ask: how can Obama, such a brilliant student of American law, politics, and culture, not get the joke — or at least not recognize that the joke was on *his enemies*?

But then I realized I had failed to account for what can be called the Harvard Factor. The presumptive Democratic presidential nominee had, after all, been elected to the staff of the *Harvard Law Review* in the late 1980s and assumed the presidency of that august publication in 1990. By that time, the strictures of political correctness had seeped into all levels of American higher education and had utterly destroyed the sense of humor of so many college and university students. At the very least, this atmosphere stifled them from admitting (to anyone but their friends) that they even *got* a joke involving matters of gender, race, sexual orientation, religion, or any other hot-button issue at the center of the nation's culture wars. And, as was predictable, the intellectual rot that began to infect the academy in the mid 1980s spread to the "real world" within a single generation. All of this displaced outrage, by Obama and many of his supporters, suddenly made sense.

The Harvard factor

Interestingly, it was Harvard Law School, regarded by many as the apex of legal education (and located in the heart of liberal Cambridge) that early grappled with the appropriateness of punishing students for engaging in satire and parody. With the eyes of the higher-education elite watching, the fabled law school established, in the early '90s, that a written parody poking fun at a female member of the academic community is no different than punishable "sexual harassment."

The campus came to a near-standstill in 1992 — just one year after Obama had graduated — over a piece in the *Harvard Law Review*'s annual April Fool's Day issue, the *Harvard Law Revue*. In this parody, meant for circulation only among *Law Review* members, the editors mocked the scholarship of then–recently deceased New England School of Law professor Mary Joe Frug, who had been tragically stabbed to death near her Cambridge residence. At the time of her gruesome death, Frug was working on a comprehensive treatment of feminist legal philosophy, in which she insisted that the contemporary legal system "constructs" women's sex and gender roles, and that rules permit not only the "sexualization" of the female body, but also its "terrorization." Her arguments, it could be (and was) reasonably argued, bordered on the bizarre, and her prose was laced with expletives. The majority of the *Harvard Law Review*'s editors nonetheless favored publishing the unfinished draft of her work as a tribute to Frug. A vocal minority opposed the decision, arguing that the draft was sloppy and that Frug herself would not have considered it ready for publication. Still others argued that Frug's theories and prose were ludicrous and did not belong in the prestigious academic journal.

For many of these reasons, a group of anonymous *Harvard Law Review* members parodied the sprawling manifesto in the annual *Law Revue*. To say the parody was scathing is an understatement: the writers made tasteless references to Frug's violent death and cruelly attributed the satirical work to "Mary Doe, Rigor-Mortis Professor of Law." Holistically, however, the piece read as a stinging rebuke of the real *Law Review*'s decision to publish Frug's unfinished draft, and more generally, an unabashed lampoon of radical-feminist scholarship — all well within the bounds of traditional parody.

As the parodic piece (leaked from what was supposed to be a small group of readers) made its rounds throughout the campus, it provoked a firestorm, particularly among faculty members and female students. The president of the *Law Review* wrote an open letter apologizing to the offended parties. The editors originally responsible for publishing Frug's actual manifesto also apologized for not protesting the parody before it was printed and circulated at the annual April Fool's Day dinner of the *Law Review* staff. Finally, the authors apologized as well.

Then-dean Robert Clark initially declared that the school would not seek punitive measures. "I agree with those who think that the best response to offensive speech is not to curtail it forcibly," he said, "but to condemn it, and explain why it is wrong." Clark's response gained approval from free-speech advocates, but it did not satisfy the enraged on campus.

Professor David Kennedy pressed the school's disciplinary Administrative Board to bring charges against the parody's authors and the *Law Review*'s editors. He further recommended that the board look into whether those involved might be morally disqualified from *becoming lawyers*. Kennedy suggested, with apparent seriousness, that the piece posed a threat to women's physical safety and well-being, writing to the Board:

Many women who received this [parody] anonymously in their student box experienced the document's delivery as a direct threat of personal violence — murder of women is held out as trivial and quite palpably possible.

Remarkably, the Administrative Board appeared to agree, labeling the parody a form of "harassment." Yet it refused to punish the authors because "no law school rule imposes limits on the content of publications by students that would be applicable here." Thus, rather than absolve the accused students on grounds of academic freedom, the disciplinary body took refuge in the fact that, at that time, the law school did not have a formal code that would outlaw such a parody.

It came as no surprise when, the following year, Clark caved in to pressure and appointed a faculty committee to consider adoption of "sexual harassment guidelines." The final product was an 11-page speech code that forbade, among other things, "speech . . . or conduct of a sexual nature that (i) is *unwelcome*; and (ii) is *abusive* or unreasonably recurring or invasive; and (iii) has the purpose or effect of unreasonably interfering with an individual's work or academic performance or *creating an intimidating, demeaning, degrading, hostile, or otherwise seriously offensive working or educational environment at Harvard Law School*" [emphasis added]. This and other provisions in the code seemed directly aimed at any future repetition of humor akin to the Frug parody.

In the law school's radioactive atmosphere, even faculty members renowned for their advocacy of free speech felt the need to compromise. Professor Laurence H. Tribe, one of the nation's leading constitutional scholars, voted for the guidelines, even though one could find arguments in his authoritative 1988 treatise, *American Constitutional Law*, to vote against it. Another vociferous defender of free speech, Professor Alan Dershowitz, announced that he preferred imperfect written guidelines to the otherwise inevitable exercise of "decanal [dean's] discretion" in deciding when to punish speech transgressions. He was, in other words, voting for the guidelines to avoid far worse and unpredictable forms of censorship. This tells us much about the hurricane winds of censorship that were blowing across the Harvard campus, and just about everywhere in academia, then and now.

The authors of the Frug parody may have escaped punishment, but, with the introduction of these speech guidelines, Harvard sent a clear message: the next student to try such a stunt could be found guilty of serious charges, such as harassment and intimidation — which could prevent him or her from landing a decent job after graduation or that could even endanger obtaining a degree.

Today, the *Law Review* still puts out a written parody and conducts its annual dinner, while the Harvard Law School Drama Society produces an annual parody stage production. But none of the humor, especially that which is gender-related, has approached the frankness (or brutality, depending upon one's point of view) of the Frug parody. One can argue, of course, that this is a good thing, depending upon one's sense of the proper balance between social criticism and the need of some to be comfortable. Harvard Law, though, became undeniably *less free* than before the adoption of the guidelines.

Despite (or perhaps because of) this conscious effort on the *Law Revue*'s part to avoid controversy, its annual parody seems to become both less biting and, ironically, equally or more subject to an "insensitivity" attack every year. The same trend has affected the Drama Society. Students harshly criticized the 2006 stage parody, for example, at a tense campus forum in March of that year, citing multiple instances of negative racial stereotypes. According to the independent student-run *Harvard Law Record*, two suggestions for reform arose repeatedly at the forum, both of which reveal either a disdain for, or fundamental misunderstanding of, parody: "prohibiting the portrayal of actual students (and perhaps professors) altogether and implementing an opt-in/opt-out system whereby students could choose to be parodied or not." (In other words, you can be criticized only if you *want* to be!)

The producers of the 2006 stage show offered a public apology to those who were offended. It was "nobody's intention to hurt those parodied," they said, suggesting that even the parodists had lost sight of the function traditionally performed by parody — namely, ridicule directed to the object of scorn. "The Parody plans to take consideration of all suggestions in their re-examination of the Parody going forward," the apology stated, "and plans to address any concerns brought up by the HLS community in the future." As for the nature of the "future," that was also made clear: "Many students commented on the need for greater discussions on race, gender, and sexuality at HLS beyond the Parody context, and this open forum was a starting point for productive discussions to come." Sensitivity training, in other words, rather than biting political and social parody, was in the law school's future.

All of this mush was coming from the university that, by siring the *Harvard Lampoon* — which in turn gave the world the National Lampoon (which begot *Saturday Night Live*), Conan O'Brien, and other comedic and satirical mainstays — arguably shaped American comedy as we know it today. Given the chilly reception to parody from both administrators *and* students on today's college campuses, it is easy to see that many varieties of comedy — a treasured asset of American pop culture and a trusty tool in the crusade for free speech — could soon atrophy into irrelevancy.

The era of the *Onion*

In an age when theonion.com reportedly attracts more readers than *Newsweek*, and Jon Stewart and Stephen Colbert have become modern-day folk heroes, the political arts of parody and satire are, ironically, experiencing a renaissance among the young.

But these parodies should come with a warning label to students: don't try this on campus.

College students are encountering increasingly more trouble for using these time-tested, constitutionally protected, and, when done right, enormously effective literary devices. Students have been blacklisted by their peers, fired from campus jobs, and subjected to humiliating show trials before what can fairly be described as politicized kangaroo courts — all because of politically edgy attempts at humor that have violated the wrong person's or group's sacred cow.

In 2006, a number of students at Long Island University were fired from their resident-assistant positions because of a short film they posted on YouTube, in which they took hostage their dormitory's unofficial mascot — a rubber ducky. According to news reports, the short film, which has since been removed from YouTube, parodied Al-Qaeda hostage-kidnapping films. After a Muslim student group complained and a local news channel ran the story, the provost decided that termination was appropriate.

At Brandeis University, the humor magazine *Gravity* was accused of racism when, in April 2007, it spoofed an ad campaign for Blackberry PDA electronic devices. In the parody, a man named "BlackJerry" offered his services for three-fifths the price of the mobile device — a heavy-handed reference to the legislative apportionment compromise in the Constitution that counted a slave as three-fifths of a person. During a confrontational and often-times emotional campus forum, students accused *Gravity*'s staff of making light of slavery, thereby inflicting emotional distress upon African-American schoolmates. The blindsided humorists at first defended the ad, explaining that it was intended as a populist critique of how slavery still exists in corporate America. When this explanation did little to stem the attacks, the editorial board issued an effusive apology and agreed to demands issued by the student government, including mandatory "diversity training" sessions and the resignation of the entire editorial board, save one remaining editor who pledged to implement "a more effective editorial hierarchy" in the future, according to an article in the *Justice*, the student newspaper.

At around the same time as the *Gravity* debacle, a black student filed harassment charges against the editors of the conservative student newspaper at Tufts University, the *Primary Source*. At issue was a satirical Christmas carol, written from the point of view of an undergraduate-admissions officer, titled "O Come All Ye Black Folk," that harshly criticized race-based admissions. Muslim students followed suit, filing similar charges in response to a parody of Tufts' "Islamic Awareness Week," which pointed out unflattering but verifiably true doctrines and practices of Islam. In May, a campus disciplinary body composed of students and faculty found the newspaper guilty of "harassment" and creating a "hostile environment," and imposed editorial restrictions on the newspaper. Under pressure from free-speech advocates, including the Philadelphia-based Foundation for Individual Rights in Education (disclosure: I serve as chairman of FIRE's board), the university president lifted the penalty, but refused to vacate the finding that a violation occurred.

Similar complaints about the 2004 April Fool's Day edition at the University of Scranton resulted in the small Jesuit college shutting down the student newspaper, the *Aquinas*. According to the *Scranton Times Tribune*, the spoof included a "fictitious reference to a priest caught fooling around with a woman during the screening of *The Passion of the Christ*" and a cartoon depicting a brawl between the former and current university presidents. The university changed the door locks of the newspaper office and removed all remaining copies of the spoof from campus. According to the school's Web site, the *Aquinas* has not published an article since April 2004. University spokesman Gerry Zaboski defended the punishment by explaining that the newspaper, funded entirely by the college, was primarily an "opportunity for students really to explore and learn and apply what they have experienced in a classroom or what they may have an interest in doing in a real setting."

But one could argue that the editors of the *Aquinas* were punished for doing exactly that — applying their classroom experience and exploring a real-world career in parody. Works like *A Modest Proposal* and *King Leopold's Soliloquy* are mainstays of introductory literature classes, even at religious colleges such as Scranton, and so parody, in theory, is fully protected by academic freedom. Scranton finds itself in the awkward position of defending a punishment that Swift and Twain would have vehemently opposed. Of course, it can be argued that a religious parochial institution should have the power to control the extent to which campus publications satirize the clergy and poke fun at church doctrines. But once a religious school chooses to portray itself as devoted to the liberal arts, as Scranton has, academic freedom makes some demands that religious observance might find uncomfortable.

In truth, it is unlikely that any of the aspiring comedians and social commentators in question are all racists or misogynists. In more than one instance, the authors of an offensive or "harassing" parody were themselves members of the ethnic group they were accused of maligning. It's just that these students, raised on a television diet of *South Park* and *Family Guy*, seem to have made one crucial mistake: they thought edgy humor would be as well-received on a campus as it is on Comedy Central. The rash of free-speech controversies proves they were wrong.

For college administrators, dealing with this brand of humor is complicated by the fact that, by definition, parody requires adopting the form of the very thing it ridicules. This often leads to a basic disagreement that underlies the *New Yorker*'s Obama-cover *contretemps*: does the satire perpetuate, or ridicule, the bigotry? For example, some students accused the *Daily Princetonian* of racism in 2006 over a *faux* letter to Princeton, written in broken English, from a fictitious person named Lian Ji. The parody was clearly referring to Jian Li, the Asian-American student who filed a civil-rights complaint against the university after he was waitlisted (he eventually enrolled at Yale, and has since transferred to Harvard). Most of the editors, including a few Asian-Americans, defended the piece, writing in an open letter that "[they] embraced racist language in order to strangle it." Princeton officials didn't have much patience for this logic (the dean of student life told the *New York Times* that the editors showed "poor judgment" in publishing the parody), but unlike the University of Scranton, the school wisely allowed the controversy to run its course and did not punish the authors.

Conflating parody, harassment, and hate speech

Perhaps the greatest danger in punishing students for offensive parody is that tasteless (or even brilliant, for that matter) humor can all too easily be labeled "harassment" on our increasingly politically correct campuses. Harvard Law's Administrative Board used that term liberally in its decision. Kennedy, the self-appointed leader of the anti-parody forces, went even further and equated the parody with a "terror" attack and a "direct threat of personal violence." This thinking equates speech with action, and insult with violence — it's a classic device resorted to by the censor.

This same logical disconnect is evident in the ruling handed down by the tribunal at Tufts. The Committee on Student Life concluded that the parodic Christmas carol "targeted [black students] on the basis of their race, subjected them to ridicule and embarrassment, intimidated them, and had a deleterious impact on their growth and well-being on campus." The committee concluded that the parody of the Islamic Awareness Week flyer "targeted members of the Tufts Muslim community for harassment and embarrassment."

Under the First Amendment, the statement of a point of view, no matter how hateful, is protected speech, as long as it avoids true threats and the time, place, and manner of delivery are reasonable. If the editors of the *Primary Source* had telephoned black students repeatedly in the middle of the night and told them they were inferior, there would be a strong harassment claim. But there's no disputing that "O Come All Ye Black Folk" was, at its core, political speech, and it was delivered in a traditional manner for such speech: print.

Some have argued that the Christmas carol at Tufts went beyond critiquing affirmative action and actually made racist statements (black students are called "boisterous," for example), or that the *Harvard Law Revue* Frug piece went beyond critiquing postmodernist feminism and insulted women in general. But even if these pieces did perpetuate racist or sexist stereotypes and held certain members of the community up to ridicule, the argument that they ought to be *censored* is still far-fetched, at least as far as Supreme Court jurisprudence is concerned. Racist and sexist language — so-called hate speech — may not be pleasant, but it is nonetheless legally protected in public places governed by the Bill of Rights. Private campuses, however, are allowed to make up their own rules as to what speech is and is not acceptable. Traditionally, this separation between town and gown has made our campuses more free than the "real world," since academic freedom has long been deemed more protective of speech than mere legal requirements provide. For academic freedom to offer less protection for speech is a breathtaking departure from long-standing assumptions about the nature and purpose of the academy. As the cynics now note in Cambridge, one may not safely say in Harvard Yard what is constitutionally protected in Harvard Square. The same may be said for just about every campus where there once was a hallowed hall of learning, now converted to a humorless hall of conformity.

Hustler and the Good Reverend Falwell
While campuses may be tightening the noose on political humor, parody, in particular, has the courts' unmitigated support. In 1988, the Supreme Court decided in *Hustler v. Falwell* that the First Amendment protects a parodist or cartoonist who intentionally inflicts "emotional distress" on anyone who plays a role in American public life. In that landmark case, *Hustler* publisher Larry Flynt resorted to a fake Compari liquor ad to suggest that his ideological adversary, Reverend Jerry Falwell, had lost his virginity in a drunken encounter with his own mother in an outhouse.

"Were we to hold otherwise," wrote Chief Justice William Rehnquist, "political cartoonists and satirists" would be vulnerable to lawsuits. After all, "[t]he appeal of the political cartoon or caricature is often based on exploitation of unfortunate physical traits or politically embarrassing events — an exploitation often calculated to injure the feelings of the subject of the portrayal.

"The art of the cartoonist is often not reasoned or evenhanded, but slashing and one-sided," continued the court. The opinion went on to discuss how the weapon of humor and exaggeration was in the past directed to such figures as William M. "Boss" Tweed in New York City, and even to such notables as George Washington, Abraham Lincoln, Theodore Roosevelt, and Franklin D. Roosevelt. "From the viewpoint of history it is clear that our political discourse would have been considerably poorer without" such vicious depictions, concluded Rehnquist in a decision that has clearly become anathema on campus, and now, sadly, in the political arena. Still, the decision was unanimous and sufficiently clear, so that the issue has not been cast into doubt in any subsequent case.

Media commentators, members of the chattering classes, and the presidential candidates themselves have got to shake the politically correct bonds that have suffocated much public and political discourse in recent years. They need to invite a more liberated and intelligent public discourse, consonant with the seriousness of the challenges facing our nation. If a presidential candidate cannot — or is afraid to — admit that he sees humor as well as a political point in the kind of parodic attack (on his own critics!) represented by the *New Yorker* cover, then we are still very far from recovering from the academic plague that leaked out of the campuses in the 1980s and still inhibits free speech outside of the ivy gates. If Obama wants to be the nation's leader, he can start leading here. He needs to leave the atmosphere of censorship at the Harvard Law School and join the ranks of free men and women.

Harvey Silverglate, a Cambridge-based lawyer and writer, is co-author of The Shadow University: The Betrayal of Liberty on America's Campuses. *His forthcoming book about the Department of Justice is due from Encounter Books early in 2009. He can be reached at has@harveysilverglate.com. Jan Wolfe and Kyle Smeallie assisted in the preparation of this piece.*

APPENDIX 3

THREE FELONIES A DAY
How the Feds Target the Innocent[*]
By Harvey A. Silverglate

Introduction: Traps and Snares for the Unwary Innocent

A little over a half-century ago, an Army veteran named Joseph Edward Morissette settled in small-town Michigan to raise his family. To support his wife and young son, the 27-year-old worked as a fruit stand operator during the summer and as a trucker and scrap iron collector during the winter. His seemingly normal life came to a screeching halt, however, when he was charged with stealing from the United States government in 1952. His case would ultimately wend its way through the federal court system and end up at the Supreme Court.

One time when Morissette was out hunting for deer with his brother-in-law, he came across a heap of spent bomb casings on a tract of uninhabited land located about half a mile from a traveled road and about six miles from the main highway. To Morissette, the casings appeared abandoned. There were no signs posted to the contrary, and, having sat in a pile through several harsh Michigan winters, the casings were showing signs of rust and decomposition. When Morissette failed to bag a deer to pay for his hunting trip, he collected some of the casings, crushed them with his tractor, and sold them as scrap metal. The casings yielded him $84.

The land turned out to be Oscoda Air Base, which the military used, according to the later Supreme Court opinion, as "a practice bombing range over which the Air Force dropped simulated bombs at ground targets."[i] A police officer, likely concerned about the large amount of bomb-shaped scrap metal heaped in the bed of Morissette's truck, asked him about the casings

[*] This passage is excerpted from Harvey A. Silverglate, *Three Felonies a Day: How the Feds Target the Innocent* (New York: Encounter Books, September 2009).

and referred the matter to an FBI agent. That, in turn, led to Morissette's being indicted in federal court on the charge that he "did unlawfully, willfully and knowingly steal and convert" property of the United States in violation of a statute that provided that "whoever embezzles, steals, purloins, or knowingly converts" government property is punishable by fine and imprisonment. Morissette was convicted and sentenced to two months in prison or a fine of $200.

Morissette hadn't realized that the casings were the government's property; he had taken them on the assumption that they were abandoned. In fact, he told the police officer who first questioned him that he did not think they were of any use or that anybody would care if he took them. Yet Morissette's "innocent intention" couldn't save him at trial. Despite the facts, the trial judge forbade Morissette's lawyer to argue to the jury that his client acted with an "innocent intention," because the judge concluded that Morissette's guilt under the statute was obvious and legally irrefutable: the bomb casings were on government property, and Morissette took them without permission. It was irrelevant that Morissette might have reasonably believed the casings were abandoned property, or even that this belief was based upon the government's own failure to post a notice to the contrary. The question of whether Morissette *believed* he was not stealing, and of the government's complicity in giving him that impression, did not matter.

It's important to note that the judge's interpretation of the law departed from centuries of English common law tradition, an evolving body of judge-made interpretive law with ancient roots, based on human experience and common sense. The common law tradition, with rare and narrow exceptions, does not punish those, like Morissette, who act with innocent intent. This approach to criminal law contains a vital moral component – our society punishes only those who intentionally rather than inadvertently violate the law.[ii]

When the United States Court of Appeals for the Sixth Circuit heard Morissette's appeal in 1951, it upheld his conviction by a 2-1 vote. By the judges' stated logic, it was a "technicality" that Morissette, who they acknowledged made "no effort at concealment," never intended to steal. When it comes to statutory crimes defined by Congress, the two-judge majority argued, intent or knowledge is irrelevant unless Congress appears to provide otherwise. Morissette wisely sought, and obtained, Supreme Court review.

In its unanimous opinion, the Supreme Court threw out the appellate court's decision and, with it, Morissette's conviction.[iii] Justice Robert H. Jackson discussed the historical role of *intent* in criminal cases and "the ancient requirement of a culpable state of mind" that must accompany a culpable act. To convict one of a crime, there must be "an evil-meaning mind with an evil-doing hand" (for the technically minded, the traditional common law notion of the combination of the *actus reus* and the *mens rea*).

Based on these centuries-old requirements, Justice Jackson concluded that the courts could not presume from Congress's silence that it did away with the criminal intent requirement, as this "would conflict with the overriding presumption of innocence with which the law endows the accused." Jackson noted that, had the jurors been allowed to consider Morissette's state of mind, "[t]hey might have concluded that the heaps of spent casings left in the hinterland to rust away presented an appearance of unwanted and abandoned junk," and from that they might "have refused to brand Morissette as a thief."

Jackson and his fellow justices obviously recognized the importance of their having decided to review the Morissette case, an undertaking extended to a small minority of litigants who seek review by the high court. "This would have remained a profoundly insignificant case to all except its immediate parties," Jackson noted in the court's opinion, "had it not been so tried and submitted to the jury as to raise questions both fundamental and far-reaching in federal criminal law." And so this seemingly insignificant case had the potential to ensure the continued presence of fundamental principles of fairness and moral content in the federal criminal law. But how long would those positive developments last?

* * * * *

A few years before he wrote *Morissette v. United States*, Robert H. Jackson was serving as Franklin D. Roosevelt's new Attorney General. On April 1, 1940, Jackson assembled his cadre of chief federal prosecutors in Washington.[iv] He wanted to speak to them about a matter of grave concern—and it wasn't the evils of crime or the need to use every crime-fighting tool to the fullest. Jackson's subject, instead, was the untoward consequences of excessive prosecutorial zeal.

After explaining why a federal prosecutor must choose cases carefully and recognize that not every crime can be pursued, Jackson turned to the heart of his talk: "If the prosecutor is obliged to choose his cases, it follows that he can choose his defendants." Here one finds "the most dangerous power of the prosecutor: that he will pick people that he thinks he should get, rather than pick cases that need to be prosecuted."

Jackson was no soft touch. He knew real crimes when he saw them. After serving as Attorney General for less than two years, he would become a Supreme Court justice and serve as well as chief American war crimes prosecutor at Nuremberg. But Jackson also understood the proper limits of power and the dangerous human impulse to exert power over others. The federal law books, explained Jackson, are "filled with a great assortment of crimes," and a prosecutor "stands a fair chance of finding at least a technical violation of some act on the part of almost anyone." Prosecutors can easily succumb to the temptation of first "picking the man and then searching the law books, or putting investigators to work, to pin some offense on him."

Today, in spite of Jackson's warning, it is only a slight exaggeration to say that the average busy professional in this country wakes up in the morning, goes to work, comes home, takes care of personal and family obligations, and then goes to sleep, unaware that he or she likely committed several federal crimes that day. Why? The answer lies in the very nature of modern federal criminal laws, which have become not only exceedingly numerous (Jackson's main fear at the time of his admonition to his prosecutors) and broad, but also, since Jackson's day, impossibly vague. As the Morissette scenario indicated, federal criminal laws have become dangerously disconnected from the English common law tradition and its insistence on fair notice, so prosecutors can find some arguable federal crime to apply to just about any one of us, even for the most seemingly innocuous conduct (and since the mid-1980s have done so increasingly).

A study by the Federalist Society reported that, by the year 2003, the U.S. Code (listing all statutes enacted by Congress) contained more than 4,000 criminal offenses,[v] up from 3,000 in 1980. Even this figure understates the challenge facing honest, law-abiding citizens. Since the New Deal era, Congress has delegated to various administrative agencies the task of writing the regulations that implement many Congressional statutes. This has spawned thousands of additional pages of text that carry the same force as congressionally enacted statutes.[vi] The volume of federal crimes in recent decades has exploded well beyond the statute books and into the morass of the Code of Federal Regulations, handing federal prosecutors an additional trove of often vague and exceedingly complex and technical prohibitions, one degree removed from Congressional authority, on which to hang their hapless targets.

This development may sound esoteric to some – until they find themselves at the wrong end of an FBI investigation into, or indictment for, practices they deem perfectly acceptable. It is then that citizens begin to understand the danger posed to civil liberties when our normal daily activities expose us to potential prosecution at the whim of a government official.

How these prosecutions work and what we can do about this perilous state of affairs is the subject of this book. The dangers spelled out here do not apply only to "white-collar criminals," state and local politicians, and myriad professionals, though their stories will predominate in the chapters that follow. No field of work nor social class is safe from this troubling form of executive branch overreaching and social control, and nothing less than the integrity of our constitutional democracy hangs in the balance. After all, when every citizen is vulnerable to prosecution and prison, then there is no effective counterweight to reign in government overreaching in every sphere. The hallowed notion of "a government of laws" becomes a cruel and cynical joke.

* * * * *

When I began practicing law in 1967, I hung out my shingle as a "criminal defense and civil liberties lawyer." I linked the two practice areas because, during the turbulent '60s, it seemed that defending people accused of crime often was an exercise in the defense of freedom of speech, freedom of religion, freedom of association, or procedural due process of law. Our firm's typical cases involved what we called "the three D's": drugs, draft, and demonstrations. A few years later a large number of gender discrimination cases were added to the mix, but much of our work remained focused on the three D's.

I recognized that I made a good part of my living defending people who did very bad things (assault, robbery, murder, mayhem, larceny, and fraud, for example). Many committed the crimes charged while some did not. However, the charges against them entailed conduct that reasonable people, ordinary citizens and lawyers alike, would rightly regard as criminal, and the indictments were based on statutes that were readily understandable. One could argue that some actions should not be criminal, such as possession of marijuana, but the crimes charged were usually clearly defined.

Then, about fifteen years into my law practice, I noticed a shift in the federal courts. More and more of my clients (physicians, bankers, academics, scientists, investors, newspaper reporters, accountants, artists, and photographers [the "three D's" had by then given way to a more diverse clientele]) were being investigated and prosecuted for conduct that neither they nor I instinctively viewed as criminal. As I prepared to defend against the charges, I could not rid myself of the unsettling notion that the federal criminal laws were becoming vaguer and harder to understand with the passage of time.

This chasm between federal and state law had in theory been established long ago, in 1812, when the Supreme Court ruled in a bribery case that federal crimes were entirely creatures of congressional statute and not successors to English common law.[vii] As a result, Congress in writing statutes, and the federal courts in interpreting them, do not have the full benefit of the common law's wisdom and experience—with increasingly alarming consequences. As the Supreme Court said in 1985, "[W]hen assessing the reach of a federal criminal statute, we must pay close heed to language, legislative history, and purpose in order strictly to determine the scope of the conduct the enactment forbids."[viii] This judicial exercise, often akin to reading tea leaves, has proven disastrous. The deceptively simple exercise of divining congressional purpose in enacting a statute involves, for one thing, a dubious assumption that Congress acts with a single, much less a simple, intent. In practice, it is rarely clear what that intent was, since much federal legislation is the result of compromises that often are meant to gloss over genuine and sharp differences. For this and perhaps other reasons as well, Congress has demonstrated a growing dysfunction in crafting legislation that can in fact be understood.

As the post-New Deal regulatory and national security state took deeper root during the mid-20th century, the gulf between the defendant-protective common law tradition practiced in the states and the more malleable and prosecution-friendly federal law grew. More and more, courts departed from Justice Jackson's insistence on requiring proof of criminal intent to commit a crime, and instead subscribed to the belief that, if the nation is to be kept safe in an increasingly dangerous world, law violators must not be allowed to slip from the government's net, even when the law's prohibitions could not be understood with precision.

The danger posed by vague federal statutes was obvious to me, in part because I came of age during the era of anti-Jim Crow racial struggles in the American South. In what I now see is a historical irony, the threat back then appeared to be the abusive use of vague state breach-of-the-peace laws to turn back the wave of civil rights demonstrations in the Deep South. The 1965 Supreme Court decision *Cox v. Louisiana,*[ix] decided while I was a law student, opened my eyes to just how much mischief can be done with vague wording of the law.

In that case, Reverend B. Elton Cox, leader of a group of civil rights demonstrators, was arrested in December 1961 for violating a 1950 Louisiana criminal statute that barred picketing "in or near" courthouses. Louisiana's anti-picketing law was not a unique product of the segregated South. A similar federal statute to halt picketing of federal courthouses by

Communist sympathizers went on the books during the Red Scare era, and even northern states – notably Massachusetts and Pennsylvania – enacted similar laws.

In *Cox*, what seemed outrageous was the manner in which Louisiana officials enforced the Louisiana anti-picketing statute. Reverend Cox had made a point of getting permission from city officials to lead the demonstration across the street from the courthouse. He then led a 2,000-strong demonstration objecting to the arrest of 23 civil rights protestors the previous day. The demonstrators sang and marched peacefully until a small group of white-only lunch counter segregationists gathered nearby. Tension between the two groups escalated. The police recklessly sprayed tear gas into Reverend Cox's camp. The next day, the police arrested Cox for violating the anti-picketing law. He was sentenced to the maximum penalty of one year in jail and a $5,000 fine.

The Supreme Court summarily overturned Reverend Cox's conviction, calling the conduct of city officials "an indefensible sort of entrapment." The Court argued that the anti-picketing statute suffered from a "lack of specificity" in its mandate that demonstrations not take place "near" courthouses. Cox had received permission to lead a protest across the street – approximately 125 feet away. By telling Cox that he could lead the protest at that location but then arresting him, Louisiana officials violated his right to adequate notice and hence "due process of law." Here, the vagueness of the statute had enabled the state to mislead the citizen into running afoul of the law. *Cox* dealt a serious blow to the government's ability to pick and choose *capriciously* which citizens it will or will not prosecute and under what circumstances.

In other cases, however, the problem lay not with officials intentionally misleading citizens, but with the inherent vagueness of the statute itself. In the 1963 case, *Edwards v. South Carolina*,[x] 187 black high school and college students were convicted for "breach of the peace" during a peaceful demonstration against mistreatment of blacks. While the Supreme Court ruled the demonstration itself was protected by the First Amendment, it went further and deemed the statute unconstitutional because it was "so vague and indefinite" that it practically invited punishment of protected speech and protest. The court noted that the Supreme Court of South Carolina defined the word "peace" as used in the statute as "tranquility." "These petitioners," said the U.S. Supreme Court, "were convicted of an offense so generalized as to be, in the words of the South Carolina Supreme Court, 'not susceptible of exact definition.'"

Troublingly, the doctrines of misleading the citizen[xi] and "void for vagueness"[xii] which federal courts have applied in numerous cases with regard to state statutes, especially where states have used vague statutes to violate the federal constitutional rights of political, religious and racial minorities, have not been applied consistently or with equal rigor in federal cases, despite the modern-era explosion of vague federal criminal statutes and mountains of turgid regulations. When the Supreme Court considered an Oklahoma law that made it a crime to pay laborers less than the prevailing wage in their locality, it decided that the law's references to "locality" and "current rate of wages" left too much open to interpretation. That state law was unconstitutional, the Court determined, because its language was "so vague that men of common intelligence must necessarily guess at its meaning and differ as to" how best to comply with it.[xiii] The dangers posed by vague laws, relatively rare in modern state criminal statutes, are greatly exacerbated in the current federal criminal code. Such federal statutes have been stretched by prosecutors, often with the connivance of the federal courts, to cover a vast array of activities neither clearly defined nor intuitively obvious as crimes, both in commerce and in daily life.

I also began to notice that, as these bodies of law expanded, federal prosecutors grew more inclined to bring criminal charges for deeds that, at most, constituted arguable (sometimes *barely* arguable) civil offenses. Thus, they raised reasonably contestable federal questions that a federal court, in a civil proceeding, should have been allowed to resolve. The citizen, if wrong, would have to pay a price measured in dollars; and once the clear meaning of the statute or regulation was established, the citizen would be expected to adhere to it, next time on penalty of criminal indictment and conviction. I naively assumed that the federal courts would, by and large, insist that citizens be charged with crimes only when there was adequate notice of what constituted the crime.

I had reason, at the start of this trend, to think that the federal courts would rein in prosecutors. Consider the plight of Dorothy Garber. She ran afoul of the federal tax code, widely viewed as a confusing mishmash of arcane, complex, and often conflicting rules and interpretations. As such, tax prosecutions traditionally were to be brought only where the regulation had been sufficiently clarified so that the taxpayer could reasonably be said to have intentionally violated a known legal duty to pay taxes owed. The taxing authorities were supposed to exercise wise discretion in deciding whether to seek to collect a tax in a civil enforcement proceeding, or to seek to punish criminally a tax evader who should have known better.

Garber's case reached the Florida federal courts in the late 1970s. This taxpayer was blessed (or perhaps, under the circumstances, cursed) with a rare trait: her body manufactured an extraordinarily valuable antibody used to make blood-typing serum. She frequently sold her antibodies to a pharmaceutical company by the process of plasmapharesis, i.e., the removal, treatment, and return of blood plasma from and to her circulation, a procedure that was both uncomfortable and potentially dangerous. She underwent plasmapharesis sometimes as often as six times a month and was handsomely paid for her trouble. In 1972, she earned a weekly salary of $200. In addition, she was provided a leased automobile and a $25,000 bonus. She earned a total of $87,200 that year, and nearly as much in each of the two previous years.

Garber failed to report as income any of this money except her weekly $200 salary. Consequently, she was charged with criminal tax evasion. Her defense was intriguing, more a reflection of the conundrum of the federal tax code perhaps than of her alleged dishonesty. Examples of non-taxable transactions, some of which produce monetary gains, are found scattered throughout the tax code in various contexts. For example, if one owns some physical item, a "capital asset," and sells that asset for one's cost, however calculated, there is no taxable gain. If one is injured in an accident, compensation for pain and suffering is not taxable, in contrast to compensation for lost wages. These special categories of assets and of revenue, many of which get quite technical, often confound even the most experienced tax lawyers and accountants.

Garber, a lay person, argued that her body was a "capital asset" under the Internal Revenue Code, and that when she sold a portion of that asset, the sale was a non-taxable exchange because the tax cost basis of the asset with which she parted, i.e. her blood plasma, was precisely equal to the funds she received. The funds merely replaced the plasma she gave to the laboratory and therefore were neither proceeds of a business nor payment for services, either of which would render the proceeds taxable as "earned income."

The United States Court of Appeals for the Fifth Circuit saw the issue as "a unique legal question,"[xiv] noting that Garber testified "that she thought, after speaking with other blood donors, that because she was selling a part of her body, the money received was not taxable." The trial judge had told the jury that monetary proceeds of such plasma donations were taxable and refused to allow Garber's defense counsel to present expert witnesses who would say otherwise.

In reversing her conviction, the Court of Appeals decided not only that she had a right to present her capital exchange theory supported by expert testimony, but that "no court has yet determined whether payments received by a donor of blood or blood components are taxable as income." If Garber performed a service, it was taxable; if, on the other hand, "blood plasma, like a chicken's eggs, a sheep's wool, or any salable part of the human body," is tangible property, then her revenues were not taxable. Most importantly, the court declared that, because the law was vague and unsettled, "a *criminal* proceeding…is an *inappropriate vehicle* for pioneering interpretations of tax law."[xv] In other words, the government should have brought a civil action against Garber to seek collection of the tax owed, not a criminal one to punish her.

Today, the Justice Department encourages federal prosecutors to do exactly what the *Garber* court condemned. In particular, federal prosecutors' novel use of long-standing but utterly formless "anti-fraud" laws, which cover increasingly vast areas of American life, threaten honest (and apparently law-abiding) business executives and other professionals, as well as other ordinary citizens. In 2003, Michael Chertoff, then second in command of the Justice Department's Criminal Division, even went so far as to boldly declare that federal prosecutors should exploit anti-fraud provisions to indict business executives because "criminal prosecution is a spur for institutional reform."[xvi]

The federal government's preference for criminal prosecutions (over either civil prosecution or "institutional reform" via the legislative branch) to expand the reach of the law is not limited to vague "anti-fraud" statutes and regulations. The same can be said for other now commonly used statutes – conspiracy, bribery, and extortion, among others. Even the most intelligent and informed citizen (including lawyers and judges, for that matter) cannot predict with any reasonable assurance whether a wide range of seemingly ordinary activities might be regarded by federal prosecutors as felonies.

* * * * *

The trend of ambitious prosecutors exploiting vague federal laws and pursuing criminal charges instead of oftentimes more appropriate civil actions, something that they could not readily get away with in many state courts, has been alarming enough, but it's not the whole story. Indeed, the threat posed by federal prosecutors has become a veritable perfect storm lately, due to the convergence of this trend with the commonplace legal tactics that these prosecutors wield in order to get convictions in the vast majority of cases. Prosecutors are able to structure plea bargains in ways that make it nearly impossible for normal, rational, self-interest calculating people to risk going to trial. The pressure on innocent defendants to plead guilty and "cooperate" by testifying against others in exchange for a reduced sentence is enormous – so enormous that such cooperating witnesses often fail to tell the truth, saying instead what prosecutors want to hear. As Harvard Law School professor Alan Dershowitz has colorfully put it, such cooperating defendant-witnesses "are taught not only to sing, but also to compose."[xvii]

[i] *Morissette v. United States*, 342 U.S. 246, 247-250 (1952); further details available from the Court of Appeals opinion affirming Morissette's conviction, *Morissette v. United States*, 187 F.2d 427 (6th Cir. 1951).
[ii] See, generally, Ford W. Hall, *The Common Law: An Account of Its Reception In the United States*, 4 VAND. L. REV. 791 (1951).
[iii] Justice Douglas concurred in the result without signing onto Justice Jackson's opinion, and Justice Minton took no part in the decision of the case.
[iv] Robert Jackson, "The Federal Prosecutor," April 1, 1940, delivered at the second Annual Conference of United States Attorneys, in Washington, D.C., reproduced at 31 AM. INST. CRIM. L. & CRIMINOLOGY 3 (1940-1941).
[v] John S. Baker, Jr., *Measuring the Explosive Growth of Federal Crime Legislation*, Federalist Society for Law and Public Policy Studies White Paper, May 2004, available at http://www.fed-soc.org/doclib/20070404_crimreportfinal.pdf. The Federalist Society commissioned this study, the report says, "to ascertain the current number of crimes in the United States Code, and to compare that figure against the number of federal criminal provisions in years past." The report analyzed legislation enacted between 1997 through 2003.
[vi] When Congress enacts a general statute, it sometimes assigns to some administrative agency the authority to write detailed or explanatory regulations that put flesh on the statutory skeleton. Thus, the federal statute that outlaws securities fraud assigns to the Securities and Exchange Commission the authority to write regulations detailing various kinds of securities fraud. Violation of a regulation thus becomes the equivalent of violation of the underlying statute.
[vii] See *United States v. Hudson & Goodwin*, 11 U.S. (7 Cranch) 32 (1812) (unlike state courts, federal courts cannot exercise common law criminal jurisdiction); *Erie R. Co. v. Tompkins*, 304 U.S. 64 (1938) (there is no general federal common law, even in civil matters); *Whalen v. U.S.*, 445 U.S. 684, 698 (1980) (the power to define crimes and punishments "resides wholly with the Congress"); *Dixon v. United States*, 126 S.Ct. 2437, 2439 (2006) ("Federal crimes are solely creatures of statute") (citing *Liparota v. United States*, 471 U.S. 419, 424 (1985)). This may have been because "[t]he Framers … recognized that the diverse development of the common law in the several States made a general federal reception impossible." *Seminole Tribe of Florida v. Florida*, 517 U.S. 44, 139-140 (1995) (Souter, J., dissenting).
[viii] *Dowling v. U.S.* 473 U.S. 207, 213 (1985).
[ix] *Cox v. Louisiana*, 379 U.S. 536 (1965).
[x] *Edwards v. South Carolina*, 372 U.S. 229 (1963).
[xi] See *Cox v. Louisiana*, 379 U.S. 559 (1965); *Raley v. Ohio*, 360 U.S. 423 (1959).
[xii] See *Papachristou v. City of Jacksonville*, 405 U.S. 156 (1972); *Edwards v. South Carolina*, 372 U.S. 229 (1963).
[xiii] *Connally v. General Construction Co.*, 269 U.S. 385, 391 (1926).
[xiv] *United States v. Garber*, 607 F.2d 92 (5th Cir. 1979) (*en banc*).
[xv] *Id.* (emphasis added).
[xvi] Proceedings of the 17th Annual National Institute on White Collar Crime, March 6, 2003, quoted in John Gibeaut, *Junior G-Men*, 89 A.B.A. J. 46, 48 (June 2003).
[xvii] Prof. Dershowitz has used this formulation on numerous occasions in his Harvard Law School classes. See Harvey A. Silverglate, "Ashcroft's big con: False confessions, coerced pleas, show trials — the Justice Department's reliance on Soviet-style tactics has turned the war on terror into a Potemkin village," *THE BOSTON PHOENIX*,, June 25, 2004, available at http://bostonphoenix.com/boston/news_features/top/features/documents/03936976.asp. See also Paul Craig Roberts, "Fake Crimes," Feb. 4, 2004, available at http://www.lewrockwell.com/roberts/roberts29.html.

Mr. SCOTT. Thank you.
Ms. Willard?

TESTIMONY OF NANCY WILLARD, M.S., J.D., DIRECTOR, CENTER FOR SAFE AND RESPONSIBLE INTERNET USE, EUGENE, OR

Ms. WILLARD. Thank you very much.

I have prepared and provided you a joint statement of opposition to the Megan Meier cyberbullying bill signed by every author of a book on cyberbullying in the United States, as well as many other risk-prevention professionals. This bill will not effectively address cyberbullying, for many of the reasons which you already outlined.

[The information referred to follows:]

Joint Statement on the Megan Meier's Cyberbullying Prevention Act, HR 6123

Submitted to:
The Subcommittee on Crime, Terrorism, and Homeland Security
Committee on The Judiciary
House of Representatives
September 30, 2009

The undersigned represent the leading nationally recognized researchers and authorities on the issue of cyberbullying. Collectively, our purpose in releasing this statement is to express our professional opinion that Megan Meier's Cyberbullying Prevention Act is a well-meant, but faulty, vehicle for addressing this serious social problem.

In no way is our objection founded upon a belief that cyberbullying is not significant enough to warrant action. Clearly, cyberbullying causes serious emotional and academic damage to victims. It is our concern for the children involved in these behaviors that prompts our objection to the proposed legislation. Although the proposed legislation has raised free speech concerns, our statement will not address those concerns. Our disagreement is grounded in our comprehensive understanding of the phenomenon of electronic aggression and our belief that this legislation will be ineffective in addressing the fundamental causes and correlates of the problem, and further, may in fact provide a distraction from the need for better, more effective prevention and intervention efforts.

Cyberbullying is a complex issue that involves education, emotional development, and social relationships. Although cyberbullying may appear to be as simple as cruel electronic messages, in fact research has clearly shown it to frequently be part of a pattern of offline and online harassment. The complexity of these behaviors cannot, unfortunately, be addressed by simply declaring them illegal. While such legislation is often defended as merely a beginning in addressing complex behaviors, it may in fact serve to distract stakeholders from investing in the comprehensive, ongoing, in-depth prevention and intervention efforts that are needed to truly prevent such trauma.

When it comes to children victimizing other children, the research has consistently demonstrated that both aggressors and targets in electronic aggression situations have significant psychosocial concerns. Further, a child who is victimized repeatedly and cruelly in school may, out of depression and despair, retaliate with cyberbullying and under this legislation would be branded a criminal, not a victim. As professionals, we see such behavior as more appropriately addressed though comprehensive efforts to establish school communities where every student feels supported, and where bullying and aggression of any kind is not allowed. These are issues that must be addressed locally in schools and with children's caregivers, rather than by the federal government.

Our objection to this legislation should not be misconstrued as dismissive of the importance of the need to proactively address the concerns of cyberbullying. To effectively address these concerns will require comprehensive funding of the safe schools and communities programs in states, districts, and local communities, with a specific directive that schools and communities must mobilize to address the new risks to young people presented by new technologies.

Submitted by:
Nancy Willard, M.S., J.D. Director Center for Safe and Responsible Internet Use. Author of Cyberbullying and Cyberthreats: Responding to the Challenge of Online Social Aggression, Threats and Distress.
Website: http://csriu.org/cyberbully.

Patti Agatston, Ph.D, Licensed Professional Counselor. Co-author of Cyber Bullying: Bullying in the Digital Age, Cyber Bullying, A Prevention Curriculum for Grades 3-5, Cyber Bullying, A Prevention Curriculum for Grades 6-12.
Website: http://www.cyberbullyhelp.com.

Robin Kowalski, Ph.D, professor of Psychology at Clemson University. Author and co-author of Complaining, Teasing, and Other Annoying Behaviors, Social Anxiety, Aversive Interpersonal Behaviors, Behaving Badly, and The Social Psychology of Emotional and Behavioral Problems, Cyber Bullying: Bullying in the Digital Age, Cyber Bullying, A Prevention Curriculum for Grades 3-5, Cyber Bullying, A Prevention Curriculum for Grades 6-12.
Website: http://www.cyberbullyhelp.com.

Sameer Hinduja, Ph.D., is an assistant professor of criminology and criminal justice at Florida Atlantic University. Co-author of Bullying Beyond the Schoolyard: Preventing and Responding to Cyberbullying.
Website: http://www.cyberbullying.us.

Justin W. Patchin, Ph.D., is an assistant professor of criminal justice at the University of Wisconsin—Eau Claire. Co-author of Bullying Beyond the Schoolyard: Preventing and Responding to Cyberbullying.
Website: http://www.cyberbullying.us.

Elizabeth K. Englander, Ph.D. is Director, Massachusetts Aggression Reduction Center and Professor of Psychology at Bridgewater State College
http://webhost.bridgew.edu/marc/

Barbara C. Trolley, PhD, CRC, Professor, St Bonaventure University, Co-author of Demystifying and Deescalating Cyber Bullying: A resource guide for counselors, educators, and parents, Cyberkids (in press), Cyberbullying and Cyberbalance (in press) and Browser the mouse and his internet adventure: Browser learns about cyberbullying and making a safety plan (in press).

Stan Davis, school counselor, consultant, and author of Schools Where Everyone Belongs and Empowering Bystanders in Bullying Prevention.
http://www.stopbullyingnow.com/

Christopher J. Ferguson, Ph.D.
Department of Behavioral, Applied Sciences and Criminal Justice
Texas A&M International University

For more information, contact Nancy Willard.
Email: nwillard@csriu.org
Cell: 541-556-1145

Ms. WILLARD. We also acknowledge the good intentions of Ms. Wasserman Schultz in addressing this through education, but we have significant concerns about this bill as currently drafted. So I would like to go into those.

First of all, we have to understand that there is a lot of mistaken understanding in this area. In fact, the Lori Drew-Megan Meier case was inaccurately reported. Lori did not create that profile, she did not engage in or direct the communications, and she wasn't even home when the harmful communications were sent. My information comes from the prosecutor in the community who presented at a MAG conference that I presented at.

One in five teens have not been sexually solicited by adult sexual predators. That was primarily teen-on-teen sexual harassment, which they handled effectively. The incidence of online predation in 2006, from Crimes Against Children Research Center, was around 600 incidents, about 1 percent of all arrests for sexual abuse of minors.

We have a significant amount of techno panic going on here. And until we get to an accurate understanding of the actual risks, we are not going to proceed effectively. So the actual risks include electronic aggression. I was going to say more, but, Mr. Scott and Mr. Gohmert, you have a great understanding of these issues.

Risky sexual personal relationship issues. There is sexual solicitation going on. It is primarily among teens. We have unsafe cyberdating. Abusive partners are using this technology for control. And we have the sexting issue.

We also have issues that haven't even percolated up in our understanding. Unsafe communities, where kids are encouraging self-harm, anorexia, self-cutting; and also dangerous groups, online gangs and hate groups. And, Mr. Scott, we could do some amendments to your really excellent "PROMISE Act" to address some of these issues.

The research has indicated that the young people who are at greater risk in the offline world are at greater risk online. These issues involved incidents between known peers. The majority of young people are actually making good choices online. And teens whose parents are actively and positively engaged are engaging in less-risk behavior.

We have to stop the negativity that we have, the fear, the kind of "reefer madness," "just say no" approach to these issues. To address these, we have a three-part program that we need to be doing.

We need to make sure that we have Web 2.0 technologies in schools, because we can't teach kids how to swim unless we get the swimming pools in school, okay? One of the major barriers to doing that is the fear that is generated about youth risk online that is grounded in an inaccurate understanding of these risks.

In risk prevention, we look at things from a universal approach and a targeted approach. We need universal digital safety and media literacy in schools. Some of the challenges include: A lot of the curriculum that out there is this "reefer madness," "just say no" approach. And there is a lack of accurate understanding among teachers.

But this new requirement to the "Children's Internet Protection Act" is causing a shift. Schools are mobilizing to address these issues, and there is new curriculum coming out that is really excellent and actually very low-cost to address these issues. We could reinforce this in the reauthorization of the "Elementary and Secondary Education Act," but, Mr. Gohmert, I do not believe there is a significant need for the funding of the creation of curriculum in this area.

The next issue is targeted youth risk prevention and intervention. We have to address these more significant risks. One of the biggest challenges is that you eliminated the block grants for State and local Safe Schools funding at exactly the time that we need to mobilize these people to address these new risks. We need to ensure that our schools are addressing youth risk online in the context of their Safe School planning.

We could have a discretionary grant program to target funds to risk prevention and intervention programs, much like what you have tried to do. But we absolutely have to have a triad of leadership in this area, not the Department of Justice in consultation with the Department of Mental Health and the Department of Education; a joint program similar to the Safe Schools and Healthy Students Program, where all three agencies are working in joint collaboration.

And we also need to recognize that there will never be evidence-based best practices in this area. It takes about a decade to get an evidence-based best practice. The research is just emerging. These technologies are changing rapidly.

There are provisions within the Safe School program to get a waiver from the principles of effectiveness if you establish an appropriate needs assessment, a plan that has a reasonable likelihood of success, and effective evaluation. So we need to tie this program to those existing requirements to ensure continuous improvement.

Thank you very much. And I have offered my assistance to your staff to seek to improve this legislation. Thank you.

[The prepared statement of Ms. Willard follows:]

PREPARED STATEMENT OF NANCY WILLARD

Testimony of:
NANCY WILLARD, M.S., J.D.
Director, Center for Safe and Responsible Internet Use
Eugene, Oregon

Before the:
Subcommittee on Crime, Terrorism, and Homeland Security
Committee on The Judiciary
House of Representatives

On:
Digital Media Safety and Literacy Education and Youth Risk Online Prevention and Intervention

September 30, 2009

Good Afternoon. Thank you for the opportunity to testify on important issues related to the safety and well-being of young people when using digital media. I would like to start with a wonderful quote from a very wise man, the honorable Richard Thornburgh set forth in the National Research Council publication, Youth, Pornography and the Internet.

> "Swimming pools can be dangerous for children. To protect them, one can install locks, put up fences, and deploy pool alarms. All of these measures are helpful, but by far the most important thing that one can do for one's children is to teach them to swim."

It is impossible to effectively teach all young people to swim if: Their parents and teachers only know how to paddle in the shallow part of the pool or are afraid to get wet. Despite the fact that they have grown up in the water and most have excellent swimming skills, they are constantly warned that water is dangerous and filled with sharks. They are instructed to avoid normal swimming behavior and to tell an adult if they feel uncomfortable - but they know that many adults can't swim and fear that adults will respond by yanking them out of the pool. They can't jump into a swimming pool while at school because it is considered too risky.

Let's describe the vision for what we need to accomplish. I describe this as follows: Schools are effectively using Web 2.0 technologies to prepare students for their future education and careers, civic responsibilities, and personal life in the 21st Century. All young people understand digital media safety and literacy issues and demonstrate competence in keeping themselves safe, engaging in responsible behavior that respects the rights of others, and taking responsibility for the well-being of others. Effective risk prevention and intervention programs have been established to respond to the concerns of the minority of young people who are at greater risk of engaging in unsafe or irresponsible online behavior or victimized by others. And lastly, and filled with promise, digital technologies are effectively being used to to provide young people with information, self-help resources, adult support, peer support networks, and crisis intervention to support their health and well-being.

Fortunately, sufficient research has been conducted addressing various aspects of youth risk online that it is now possible to make preliminary conclusions about these concerns.

The young people who are in the greatest risk online are the ones who are already at greater risk in the "real world." These young people are more likely to have significant psychosocial concerns, engage in risk taking behavior, and have disrupted relations with their parents, caregivers, and other adults in their school and community. Effectively addressing these concerns will require the implementation of effective risk prevention and intervention approaches guided by mental health professionals. Sometimes, these "at risk" young people may be the victims of criminal acts or may engage in criminal behavior, thus the involvement of professionals in juvenile justice and delinquency prevention is also necessary.

Most frequently, harmful online situations involve known peers. The far more common situations include both offline and online harmful personal relationship altercations. Regardless of where young people are when they engage in harmful online interactions, the harmful impact will frequently be at school, because this is where young people are physically together. Effectively addressing these concerns will require effective school-based prevention and intervention programs.

The majority of teens appear to be generally making good choices online, report healthy responses to negative online incidents, and report that they are not distressed by these incidents. But this is a new environment in which young people are interacting and the period of childhood and adolescence is a time of exploration and risk taking. Young people are making mistakes online that can be prevented through education and adult involvement. The fact that the majority of teens are generally making good choices supports the conclusion that social norms/peer leadership risk prevention approaches will be effective. Because the majority of teens are generally making good choices and are not at risk, especially not at risk of being criminally victimized or engaging in criminal behavior, educational approaches that seek to convince them that they are at great risk and should avoid normative online behavior are worse than woefully ineffective. Such fear-based programs convince youth that adults do not understand and cannot be trusted.

Teens whose parents are both actively and positively involved in their children's online activities demonstrate the lowest levels of risky behavior online. Generating fear about Internet risk appears not to lead to greater or effective parent involvement. Parent education approaches must shift from seeking to generate fear to providing guidelines on how parents can be actively and positively involved. Parenting approaches must be determined by age, development, and risk factors of the individual child. Schools are important conduits for education and outreach to parents.

Risk prevention approaches are often divided into two types of initiatives: Universal initiatives provide education about risk concerns to the entire population. Targeted interventions are directed at those youth who are at higher risk or are engaging in higher risk behavior. This is the approach that I and other Internet safety risk prevention professionals recommend.

In order to effectively implement universal education about digital media safety and literacy it is necessary to address the essential foundation. Our schools must be using these technologies for instruction. It is impossible to prepare students for their digital media enriched future without these technologies. U.S. effectiveness and competitiveness is also dependent on this.

On top of all of the other barriers our schools face, two barriers are directly related to ineffective responses to Internet safety concerns.

The first is the misplaced reliance on filtering to manage student Internet use. Filtering is a web 1.0 protection approach - it protects against accessing objectionable material. But it is not effective in doing so when used by teens. Why? Because at the same time the federal government was requiring schools to spend millions of dollars on filtering, it was also providing funding to develop technologies that freedom fighters in countries in Asia and the Middle East can use to bypass filters and achieve anonymity. It is not possible to keep teens in electronically fenced play yards. We need more effective approaches to manage student student Internet use. But if students are engaged in relevant, exciting instruction using these technologies, misuse is much less of a concern.

The second barrier is all of the fear-mongering about youth risk online that has created the misperception that all youth are at high risk of criminal victimization when using web 2.0 interactive technologies. They are clearly not at risk. But this fear has led too many educational leaders to resist integrating the use of these technologies for instruction. So we need to delete the fear and focus on the legitimate risks, not the rare instances of criminal victimization or behavior.

To provide universal digital media safety and literacy instruction will require appropriate instructional objectives, effective curriculum and instructional approaches, and teachers who understand the issues. The Broadband Act, which has added a requirement to teach Internet safety to the Children's Internet Prevention Act has and will continue to stimulate activity in this area. There are many initiatives emerging that seek to outline instructional objectives. Effective curriculum is coming into the market place. Professional development efforts are under way.

Two current challenges are the legacy Internet safety curriculum that has been developed with funding through the Department of Justice or materials developed by state attorneys general. Much of this material is overly focused on the rare instances of criminal victimization, presents inaccurate information, and uses an ineffective "scare tactics" instructional approach. What we have is Reefer Madness and "Just say 'no'" revisited. This kind of curriculum teaches young people not to trust adults.

The second barrier is the significant degree of professional development that is necessary. Of particular importance is raising the level of understanding of health educators and counselors, whose instructional involvement is essential. It is not appropriate for our educational technology staff to teach about risky sexual online concerns.

My recommendations to address universal digital media safety and literacy education are to ensure that there are requirements to do so as part of school planning by incorporating this requirement into the Elementary and Secondary Education Act. Thus, in addition to the incentive provided by the Broadband Act, this would stimulate multidisciplinary planning. Congress could also provide discretionary grants to state and local education agencies to stimulate innovative curriculum and instruction. I do not recommend federal funding of digital media safety and literacy curriculum. Development of this curriculum is best left to the private sector.

To address youth risk online will require effective prevention and intervention strategies. We will have to accomplish these in a new way however. Traditional risk prevention requires the implementation of evidence-based best practices. There are not evidence-based best practices to address youth risk online and will likely never be any. The research insight is still emerging. And the digital technologies and ways in which they are used continue to rapidly change. It can take a decade to conduct the research, develop a program, obtain funding, implement the program, collect and assess the data, write and publish the results.

What we must do is shift to a continuous improvement model. Fortunately, there is already statutory guidance on how to do this. In the safe schools program there is a provision that allows grantees to seek a waiver of the Principles of Effectiveness requirement to respond to new challenges. To obtain a waiver requires an effective statement of the problem, a strategic plan, evidence of likelihood of success, and an evaluation plan.

The major challenge in this area is the decision not to seek funding for the state and local safe school programs, Title IV. It is my understanding that this program is being redesigned, which is good. But it is essential to retain the critical state and school safe school infrastructure to address these new concerns.

My recommendations to effectively address youth risk online are as follows: Restore structural funding to the state and local safe schools programs. In the reauthorization of ESEA, require the development of safe school plans that address these new risks. Establish a new discretionary grant program that emulates the multidisciplinary approach of the Safe Schools/Healthy Students program, that is a program that is jointly coordinated by the Department of Mental Health, Department of Education, and Office of Juvenile Justice and Delinquency Prevention. Funding initiatives under this program could be directed at community mental health programs, school-based programs, and programs to address criminal victimization or behavior. Funding for professional development initiatives and for programs that use digital media for the delivery of risk prevention and intervention should also be supported. This new grant program would fund well-designed, innovative projects that have a strong evaluation component.

With respect to the legislation currently before this Subcommittee, I have attached a statement of opposition to HR 6123 that has been signed by all of this nation's leading authorities on the issue of cyberbullying. While we agree that attention must be paid to this new concern, trying to make this a federal criminal offense is ludicrous for the reasons we have outlined.

The current approach of the Wasserman-Schultz Adolescent Web Awareness Requires Education Act is entirely unacceptable for two reasons.

The first reason is that the sole focus of this legislation is on the rare instances of Internet crime. This bill would perpetuate the misunderstanding and fear that young people are at high risk of criminal victimization when online, which simply is not the case. Curriculum that seeks to impart such misunderstanding and fear would be rejected by young people, cause young people to distrust adults, and would not lead to more effective parenting around these issues. The delivery of such curriculum would greatly diminish the opportunities for schools to shift to 21st Century instruction using these interactive technologies, thus harming U.S. effectiveness and competitiveness, and impairing the ability of U.S. students to be effective and productive citizens.

The second concern is directing funding to the Department of Justice. While DOJ clearly must be involved in addressing these concerns, there is a far greater need to mobilize the mental health and education communities. A three-part partnership is necessary, with the vast majority of the funds disseminated to grantees whose programs are aligned with the Departments of Mental Health and Education.

Thank you for the opportunity to discuss these issues with you.

ATTACHMENT

Digital Media Safety and Literacy
Youth Risk Online Prevention and Intervention
Research Insight - Challenges - Recommendations

Nancy E. Willard, M.S., J.D.
Center for Safe and Responsible Internet Use
September 30, 2009[1]

This White Paper will outline current insight into issues of youth risk online and set forth recommendations for strategies to address the concerns. The Internet and other digital technologies clearly have had a profound, beneficial impact on society. There are, however, concerns associated with the use of these digital technologies by young people. Collaborative, multidisciplinary prevention and intervention approaches are necessary to address these new concerns. Further, all young people (and adults) need guidance on a range of digital media safety and literacy issues.

Research and Analysis

Swimming Pools

Let's start the discussion with a wise statement made by the Honorable Dick Thornburgh, former U.S. Attorney General, in the preface to the National Research Council report, *Youth Pornography and the Internet*.

> "Swimming pools can be dangerous for children. To protect them, one can install locks, put up fences, and deploy pool alarms. All of these measures are helpful, but by far the most important thing that one can do for one's children is to teach them to swim."[2]

It is impossible to effectively teach all young people to swim if ...

- Their parents and teachers only know how to paddle in the shallow part of the pool or are afraid to get wet.
- Despite the fact that they have grown up in the water and most have excellent swimming skills, they are constantly warned that water is dangerous and filled with sharks.
- They are instructed to avoid normal swimming behavior and to tell an adult if they feel uncomfortable - but they know that many adults can't swim and fear that adults will respond by yanking them out of the pool.
- They can't jump into a swimming pool while at school because it is considered too risky.

Vision

- Schools are effectively using Web 2.0 technologies to prepare students for their future education and careers, civic responsibilities, and personal life in the 21st Century.
- All young people understand digital media safety and literacy issues and demonstrate competence in ...
  - Keeping themselves safe.
  - Engaging in responsible behavior that respects the rights of others.
  - Taking responsibility for the well-being of others.
- Effective risk prevention and intervention programs have been established to respond to the concerns of the minority of young people who are at greater risk of engaging in unsafe or irresponsible online behavior or victimized by others.

---

2 Thornburgh, D. & Lin, H. (2002) *Youth, Pornography and the Internet*. National Academy of Sciences. http://www.nap.edu/openbook.php?isbn=0309082749.

- Digital technologies are effectively being used to to provide young people with information, self-help resources, adult support, peer support networks, and crisis intervention to support their health and well-being.

Overview of Research Findings, Risk Prevention Insight, and Recommendations

Fortunately, sufficient research has been conducted addressing various aspects of youth risk online that it is now possible to make preliminary conclusions about these concerns. More research is clearly necessary. Harvard's Berkman Center for Internet and Society hosted the Internet Safety Technical Task Force, which issued a report in January 2009.[3] As part of this report, this nation's leading researchers on youth risk online, who prepared a Literature Review of known research concerning children's online safety. The following material is grounded in research insight and has been informed by the perspectives of professionals who focus on these concerns.[4]

- The young people who are in the greatest risk online are the ones who are already at greater risk in the "real world."[5] These young people are more likely to have significant psychosocial concerns including depression, anxiety, anger, and suicidal ideation, engage in offline risk taking behavior, be victims of physical and sexual abuse and engage in physical and sexual aggression, have friends who are also "at risk," and have disrupted relations with their parents, caregivers, and other adults in their school and community. However, research is also indicating that some young people who do not demonstrate risk factors are also engaging in risky or irresponsible online behavior. This concern is not yet fully understood. It may relate to the negative influences on online behavior, including anonymity, lack of tangible feedback, and online group dynamics.
  - Effectively addressing these concerns will require the implementation of effective risk prevention and intervention approaches guided by mental health professionals. Sometimes, these "at risk" young people may be the victims of criminal acts or may engage in criminal behavior, thus the involvement of professionals in juvenile justice and delinquency prevention is also necessary. There are currently no evidence-based risk prevention and intervention programs to address these new concerns, but insight from existing effective programs can be applied. New prevention and intervention programs that use digital media technologies appear to hold exciting promise.
- Most frequently, harmful online situations involve known peers.[6] The "stranger danger" warnings in Internet safety messages are not supported by the research. The far more common situations include both offline and online harmful personal relationship altercations. The vast majority of these harmful interactions are occurring in digital environments where there are no responsible adults present. Regardless of where young people are when they engage in harmful online interactions, the harmful impact will frequently be at school, because this is where young people are physically together.
  - Effectively addressing these concerns will require school-based prevention and intervention programs that help students build positive personal relationships, empower peers to effectively assist in resolving minor incidents, encourage students to report incidents they witness or are involved in to adults, and ensure that adults know how to effectively intervene to assist all youth involved to resolve the incident in a safe, respectful, and healthy manner.
- In repeated studies, the majority of teens appear to be generally making good choices online, report healthy responses to negative online incidents, and report that they are not distressed by these incidents.[7] The extensive amount of fear about young people online is not supported by the research data. Unfortunately, terms such as "dangerous and disturbing," "exceptionally risky," "socially deviant," are often used to describe youth online activities by the organizations publicizing survey data in an

---

3 http://cyber.law.harvard.edu/research/isttf.

4 The author of this report regularly communicates with a loosely organized collaborative of researchers, risk prevention professionals, Internet safety advocates, educational technology professionals, librarians, law enforcement, and industry leaders who focus on Internet safety. The purpose of this multidisciplinary collaborative is to identify and encourage effective education, prevention, and intervention approaches to address all areas of digital media safety and literacy.

5 Wolak, J., Finkelhor, D., Mitchell, K., & Ybarra, M. (2008) Online "Predators" and their Victims: Myths, Realities and Implications for Prevention and Treatment. *American Psychologist*, 63, 111-128. http://www.unh.edu/ccrc/internet-crimes/papers.html; The December 2007 Supplement of the *Journal of Adolescent Health*, Youth Violence and Electronic Media: Similar Behaviors, Different Venues? http://www.jahonline.org/content/suppl07 contains several articles that document the association of psychosocial concerns and cyberbullying.

6 Wolak, J., Mitchell, K., and Finkelhor, D. (2006). Online victimization of youth: Five years later. *National Center for Missing & Exploited Children Bulletin* - #07-06-025. Alexandria, VA http://www.unh.edu/ccrc/internet-crimes/papers.html; McQuade, S. (2008) *Study of Internet and At Risk Behaviors*; http://www.prweb.com/releases/Cyber_Safety/Ethics_Initiative/prweb1035784.htm.

7 All of the studies cited in this section.

apparent attempt to generate news coverage. Often these surveys do not reflect a high degree of academic rigor. Sometimes, these terms are applied to normative online or teen behavior that could be associated with risk, but is not inherently risky. Other times, these terms are used when the data itself demonstrates a small percentage of young people report engaging in concerning behavior. Numerous studies also document that the majority of teens are not reporting negative incidents to adults. In the majority of situations, youth report that they effectively resolved the problem. But they also apparently fear the consequences of reporting online concerns to adults, especially adult overreaction and loss of access.

- This is a new environment in which young people are interacting and the period of childhood and adolescence is a time of exploration and risk taking. Young people are making mistakes online that can be prevented through education and adult involvement. All young people need greater insight into the risks, protective strategies, and standards for responsible behavior. The fact that the majority of teens are generally making good choices supports the conclusion that social norms/peer leadership risk prevention approaches will be effective. Because the majority of teens are generally making good choices and are not at risk, educational approaches that seek to convince them that they are at great risk and should avoid normative online behavior are worse than woefully ineffective. Such fear-based programs convince youth that adults do not understand and will overreact to any report of concern - that adults cannot be trusted.

- Teens whose parents are both actively and positively involved in their children's online activities demonstrate the lowest levels of risky behavior online.[8] Unfortunately, many parents appear to be "clueless" about their children's online activities. Parents are generally more concerned than their teens about potential online risks. There appears to be no correlation between the degree to which parents express concerns about online risks and their level of attention to their child's online activities. In other words, generating fear about Internet risk appears not to lead to greater parent involvement.
  - Parent education approaches must shift from seeking to generate fear to providing guidelines on how parents can be actively and positively involved. Parenting approaches must be determined by age, development, and risk factors of the individual child. Children should use the Internet in safer places. The pre-teen and early teen years require effective parent involvement, as young people start to engage in social networking environments. Older teens should be expected to be independent. Young people who are at greater risk online require greater supervision. But unfortunately, a focus on parents of the more vulnerable youth may not be entirely effective, because these parents are the least likely to be effectively involved with their children. Parents who are effectively involved should be encouraged to encourage their children to be peer leaders who provide assistance to their peers and report significant concerns to responsible adults. Schools are important conduits for education and outreach to parents.

Universal & Targeted Risk Prevention

Risk prevention approaches are often divided into two types of initiatives: Universal (Primary) and Targeted (Secondary) prevention.[9] This approach has been followed in this White Paper.

- Universal initiatives provide education about risk concerns to the entire population in a manner that will seek to influence those youth who are potentially at higher risk.
- Targeted interventions are directed at those youth who are at higher risk and are engaging in higher risk behavior.

Digital Media Safety and Literacy - Universal Education

All young people must gain insight and understanding of a wide range of digital media safety and literacy issues. Many educators are currently outlining recommended scope and sequence for instructional objectives in this arena. A high degree of creativity should be encouraged at this time because out of such creativity will emerge greater and more comprehensive understandings. The following is the outline of issues currently set for by the Center for Safe and Responsible Internet Use:

---

8 Rosen, L. D., et al., (2008) The association of parenting style and child age with parental limit setting and adolescent MySpace behavior, *Journal of Applied Developmental Psychology*. doi:10.1016/j.appdev.2008.07.005. Rosen based his analysis on the types of parenting originally identified by Diane Baumrind. Authoritative parents are active and positive.

9 Sometimes, this is referred to as primary, secondary, and tertiary or universal, selected and targeted.

Core Competencies

- Making good choices online. Critical thinking and effective problem-solving in an environment where there is the ability to achieve anonymity, but also the potential for widespread dissemination of material, lack of tangible feedback of consequences of online actions, and online group dynamics that can foster healthy or unhealthy behavior that has a powerful impact. Assisting others who are being harmed online or reporting to a responsible adult.
- Information credibility. Assessing the credibility and accuracy of material found online or presented electronically. Recognizing common techniques used to influence attitudes and behavior.
- Keeping life in balance. Keeping use of digital media in balance with other important life activities.
- Protecting personal information and reputation. Being mindful of the prospect that any information disseminated in an electronic format can become public and permanent and guiding all disclosure accordingly. Knowing how to protect different kinds of personal information and images, including contact, financial, and other.
- Interacting safely with others. Interacting safely with friends, acquaintances, friends of friends, and strangers in various electronic communication environments.

Sites and Technologies

- Internet use agreements. Understanding and recognizing the need to abide by the terms of Internet use agreements, including school, employer, sites, and services. Recognizing the reason for common restrictions.
- Computer security. Knowing how to keep digital devices secure from malware.
- Scams. Recognizing and avoiding scams that seek personal and financial information, could lead to security concerns, and other harm.
- Accidental access of objectionable material, most notably pornography. Implementing technical protections and using effective surfing strategies to limit accidental access.
- Empowered consumption in an era of behavioral targeting. Recognizing how sites engage in behavioral targeting by creating market profiles and using this information to target advertising. Recognizing other forms of online advertising, including advergaming, permission marketing, and viral marketing.
- Protective features. Knowing how to use protective safety features to limit access to personal information, ensure appropriateness of material posted on profile, safely add or block others, and report abuse.

Digital Media Literacy - Consuming, Creating, Collaborating, and Convincing in Web 2.0

- Free speech. Understanding the free speech protections and the boundaries of responsible speech.
- Accurate attribution. Recognizing that effective attribution is essential to demonstrate respect for prior works and establish credibility. Knowing how to accurately attribute.
- Copyright and fair use. Understanding the personal and social benefits accorded by copyright protection. Knowing how to protect creative works. Respecting the copyright of others. Understanding fair use exceptions to copyright.
- Publisher responsibilities. Understanding the responsibilities related to publishing information online including appropriate attribution and respect for copyright, as well as respect for others and publishing torts including defamation and privacy rights.
- Credibility and advocacy. Knowing how to present material in an electronic medium in an manner that establishes credibility and achieves effective advocacy through persuasive writing.
- Civic collaboration. Engaging in effective collaborative efforts utilizing digital communications.

Youth Risk Online

- Electronic aggression. Effectively preventing and responding to electronic aggression. Avoiding electronic aggression. Avoiding posting material others might perceive as a threat. Reporting material that appears to indicate someone might be considering an act of violence against self or others to a responsible adult.

- Risky sexual and personal relationships concerns. Effectively preventing and responding to a range of sexual and relationship concerns including being solicited for sexual encounters, risks associated with cyberdating, use of technologies by abusive partners, and sexualized images. Avoiding harmful engagement in such activities.
- Unsafe or dangerous online groups. Recognizing and avoiding involvement in unsafe group that encourage self-harm activities, such as anorexia, self-cutting, drug or steroid use, suicide and the like, or dangerous groups, such as hate groups, gangs, hacker groups, those trafficking in pornography, and the like.

Youth Risk Online - Targeted Prevention and Intervention

There appear to be three interrelated major areas of youth risk online concerns: electronic aggression, risky sexual and relationship interactions, and unsafe or dangerous online groups. These three areas include situations where young people are engaging in activities that are placing themselves at risk or are directed at harming another. As noted, frequently, these situations involve both online and offline harmful interactions with peers.

Electronic Aggression

Cyberbullying

Cyberbullying is the use of electronic technologies to engage in repeated and/or extensively disseminated acts of cruelty towards others.[10] Cyberbullying can range from minor altercations to incidents that cause devastating emotional harm.

The different forms of cyberbullying include: Flaming, online "fights" using electronic messages with angry and vulgar language. Harassment, repeatedly sending offensive and insulting messages. Denigration, sending or posting cruel gossip or rumors about a person to damage his or her reputation or friendships. Exclusion, intentionally excluding someone from an online group, like a "buddy list." Impersonation, impersonating someone to make that person look bad, get that person in trouble or danger, or damage that person's reputation or friendships. Cyberstalking, engaging in online activities that make a person afraid for her or her safety or using technology for control in an abusive dating relationship. Outing, sharing someone's secrets or embarrassing information or images online. Trickery, tricking someone into revealing secrets or embarrassing information, which is shared or deceiving someone online to humiliate or cause harm.

The harm caused by cyberbullying may be greater than traditional bullying. Electronic aggression can be exceptionally vicious, there is no escape for the target, the harmful materials distributed more widely, the aggressor can remain anonymous, and the incidents can involve large numbers of others. Cyberbullying is resulting in school failure, school avoidance, violence, and sometimes contributing to suicide.

A review of emerging research on cyberbullying leads to the following insight:[11] Cyberbullying is a significant concern for young people. But the incident rates of cyberbullying reported in the research appear to be related to how the questions are asked. Most surveys are not yet effectively distinguishing between minor and significant incidents. The continuing incidents between known peers are causing the highest degree of distress. Addressing these incidents will be more challenging. These incidents will impact schools because they are related to on-campus bullying or could lead to retaliation at school. A significant portion of incidents appear to involve online retaliation against the person who has been aggressive at school. Both aggressors and targets appear to present significant psychosocial concerns and report involvement in offline aggression, which is more likely to occur where they are physically together at school. They also have disrupted relations with parents, which means schools will be less able to rely on parents for effective supervision, prevention and response.

The vast majority of young people are not reporting these incidents to adults. The primary reason reported for this is that young people have or feel they should be able to handle the situation on their own, which is something that should be encouraged. But many say they do not tell for fear of getting into

10 Willard, N.E. (2007) *Cyberbullying and Cyberthreats: Responding to the Challnge of Online Social Aggression, Threats, and Distress.* Research Press.

11 Youth Violence and Electronic Media: Similar Behaviors, Different Venues? *Journal of Adolescent Health.* December 2007 Supplement. http://www.jahonline.org/content/suppl07.

trouble or losing Internet access. This may, in some cases, be a legitimate concern, because their hurtful actions, online or offline, may be part of the problem. Clearly, they will not report these incidents until they have confidence that adults will be able to assist in effectively resolving the incidents.

Cyberthreats - Online Threats & "Leakage"

Another form of electronic aggression is cyberthreats.[12] Cyberthreats include direct threats or distressing material that raises concerns the person is emotionally distraught and may be considering harming someone, harming him or herself, or committing suicide. Young people make threats all the time. Their tone of voice, posture, overall interaction allow others to determine if it is a "real threat." Sometimes online material that looks threatening is just a joke. However, online threatening material can be very real.

The Federal Bureau of Investigation calls this kind of material "leakage" - when a young person intentionally or unintentionally reveals clues to feelings, thoughts, fantasies, attitudes, or intentions that may signal an impending violent act against self or others.[13] If a young person is contemplating an act of violence it is highly likely that they will be posting material online that provides strong clues to impending violence. Threat assessment and suicide prevention plans must incorporate this new understanding. Because these postings are generally made in environments where adults are not present but young people are, all young people must know how to report such concerns in their local community - and the importance of doing so.

Risky Sexual & Relationships Activities

Teens are maturing sexually and engaging in a range of sexual and personal relationship-related activities online. Much of this can be very positive. However, there are a variety of risks.

Online Sexual Predation

Much of what people think they know about online sexual predation is not supported by the research, the majority of which comes from the Crimes Against Children Research Center.[14] These incidents are very rare, just 1% of arrests for sexual abuse of minors. Predators are not targeting children. Deception about age and sexual intention is rare, however, deceptive promises of love does occur. Abduction or violence is also rare. Predators are not tracking teens based on personal contact information and abducting them. Teens meet with the predators knowing they are adults and intending to engage in sex. Many times they meet on more than one occasion. One in 5 or 7 young people have not been sexually solicited online by a dangerous adult predator. These incidents were primarily teen sexual harassment, to which the teens responded effectively. Most were not distressed. They did not report to adults because they considered the incidents "no big deal." Sexual harassment is, unfortunately, a common aspect of teen life - offline and online.

The teens who are at greatest risk of online sexual exploitation - by adults or teens, strangers or not - are those who are emotionally vulnerable, explore sexual questions in unsafe forums, post sexy images, and use sexy usernames. Boys, likely those questioning their sexual orientation, are also at risk.[11]

Pedophiles Online

Family or acquaintance abusers are using technologies for grooming or the creation of pornography. Pedophiles are also engaging with others in online communities where they rationalize their sexual activities and share child pornography.[15] The risks of sexual abuse by someone trafficking in child pornography are considered to be high.[16] Currently, there appears to be limited efforts to educate parents or risk professionals about this area of risk. Warning signs that someone may be trafficking in child pornography are likely to include addictive access, excessive secrecy, and acquisition of expensive technology and image recording equipment with no logical reason.

Unsafe Cyberdating or "Fantasy Love."

Cyberdating is, and will continue to be, a very common way for teens to form and develop relationships and can be very healthy. Of concern, is that teens might develop a "fantasy love" relationship with

---

12 Willard, Supra.

13 O'Toole, M.E. (1998) *The School Shooter: A Threat Assessment Perspective*. Federal Bureau of Investigation. http://www.fbi.gov/filelink.html?file=/publications/school/school2.pdf.

14 http://www.unh.edu/ccrc/.

15 Eichenwald, Kurt. (August 21, 2006) From Their Own Online World, Pedophiles Extend Their Reach. *New York Times*.

16 Sher, J & Kelley, (July 19, 2007) Debate on Child Pornography's Link to Molesting, *New York Times* http://www.nytimes.com/2007/07/19/us/19sex.html

someone online that is based on significant misperceptions. When "reality strikes" for one or other partner, this can lead to electronic aggression. Unfortunately, teens who are involved in cyberdating may have exchanged sexual images. If - more likely when - the relationship breaks up, these images may be distributed or there may be a threat of distribution.

Abusive Relationships.

Teens in abusive dating relationships are being controlled, threatened, and humiliated by the controlling partner through cell phones and the Internet.[17] The controlling behavior includes spreading rumors, demanding, sharing or threatening to share private or embarrassing images, and excessive text messaging to maintain control over activities and relationships.

Self-Produced Sexualized Images (Sexting)

Teens are self-producing and distributing nude sexual images, frequently via cell phone. Criminal laws against the production and dissemination for child pornography were enacted to prevent minors from being abused by adults. The application of these laws to these situations presents significant concern. This activity is frequently "courtship ritual" behavior - the new way teens are engaging in flirting and relationship building. But these situations could also be in the context of electronic aggression, sexual exploitation, abusive partnerships, trafficking in child porn, or self-initiated prostitution.

Online Pornography.

Teens may intentionally or accidentally access online pornography.[18] Most teens, especially boys, will spend some time looking. The teens at greater risk are the ones who do so excessively or are attracted to child pornography. These teens may become affiliated with groups of adult traffickers/abusers that are discussed in the section below.

Unsafe or Dangerous Online Groups

Online "communities" and web sites support unsafe activities or encourage dangerous activities. Unsafe communities support actions that can cause self-harm, including self-cutting, anorexia and bulimia, steroid use, drug use, passing-out games, suicide, and other similar unsafe activities.[19] Dangerous groups promote actions that could cause harm to others, including hate sites and groups, gangs, and other troublesome groups including groups of local youth, hacker communities, groups that exchange pornography and discuss pedophilia.[20]

These groups all appear to have similar features: Strong emotional support for marginalized youth where participants act as "mentors." Symbols that foster group identity. Online rituals that solicit evidence that the participant is truly committed to the ideals of the group. The groups exclude anyone deemed not to abide by the group norms, which acts to reinforce the importance of abiding by those norms to remain connected and receive support from the group. The group members naturalizing or rationalizing the injurious self-harm or aggressive values and behavior.

Not all online communities that vulnerable teens participate in are harmful. Marginalized youth may find a very healthy online environment where they fit in with people who have their own interests.[21] It is simply not possible to get rid of the harmful groups or try to cut off a teen's access. But because marginalized youth are attracted to online groups, the provision of online support services to such youth represents a largely untapped area of potential intervention.[22]

---

17 Picard, P. (2007) *Tech Abuse in Teen Relationships Study*. Liz Claiborne Inc. http://www.loveisnotabuse.com/surveyresults_2007mstr.htm.

18 Wolak, J., Mitchell, K., and Finkelhor, D. (2006). Online victimization of youth: Five years later. *National Center for Missing & Exploited Children Bulletin* - #07-06-025. Alexandria, VA. http://www.unh.edu/ccrc/internet-crimes/papers.htm.

19 Whitlock, J.L., Powers, J.L., Eckenrode, J., 2006. The virtual cutting edge: the internet and adolescent self-injury. *Developmental. Psychology*. 42(3), 407–417. See also, Mitchell, K. & Ybarra, M. (2007). Online behavior of youth who engage in self-harm provides clues for preventive intervention. *Preventive Medicine*, 45: 392-396. http://www.unh.edu/ccrc/internet-crimes/papers.html. Pascoe, C.J.. 2008. *"You're Just Another Fatty:" Creating a Pro-Ana Subculture Online*. Digital Youth Research http://digitalyouth.ischool.berkeley.edu/node/104. January 22, 2008.

20 Franklin, R.A., *The Hate Directory: Hate Groups on the Internet*. http://www.bcpl.net/~rfrankli/hatedir.htm; *Poisoning the Web: Hatred Online Internet Bigotry, Extremism and Violence* http://www.adl.org/poisoning_web/introduction.asp Wolf, C. (2000). *Racis(, Bigots, and the Law on the Internet*. Anti-Defamation League. http://www.adl.org/internet/internet_law1.asp; Teaching Tolerance a project of the Southern Poverty Law Clinic. *Hate on the internet*. http://www.tolerance.org/hate_internet/index.jsp; National Alliance of Gang Investigators Associations. *2005 National Gang Threat Assessment*. http://www.nagia.org/PDFs/2005_national_gang_threat_assessment.pdf.

21 Pasco, supra.

22 Pasco, supra, and Ybarra, supra.

Unsafe Posting of Material, Unsafe Interactions With Others, Addictive Access

Underlying all of the above risks are three foundational concerns. Vulnerable youth may be more apt to engage in online behavior that is more likely to lead them into dangerous situations. They may post material online, such as sexualized images, and engage in unsafe communications with others, such as discussing sexual issues with online strangers.[23] The issue is not that they are posting personal information or interacting with strangers online, which is normative online behavior. But the manner in which they are engaging in such online behaviors can place them at greater risk.

Addictive access is an excessive amount of time spent online resulting in lack of healthy engagement in other areas of life. The research on time spent involved with electronic technologies and psychosocial concerns is somewhat mixed. Some research has indicated that young people who are very active online are also very engaged in school and other activities. These are "highly social" young people who are not at risk.[24] Other research has shown a connection between an excessive amount of electronic activity and depression, social anxiety, and suicidal ideation.[25] The American Psychiatric Association recently noted that Internet addictive access appears to be a common disorder that merits inclusion in the Diagnostic and Statistical Manual of Mental Disorders as a obsessive-compulsive disorder.[26]

Challenges and Barriers

There are three approaches to address youth risk online that have been and will be ineffective. Frequently, ineffective prevention efforts are enacted or developed following the publication of misleading information related to youth risk online. This concern has come to be know as "technopanic" - a heightened degree of concern about the use of interactive technologies by young people that is inaccurate or disproportionate to the actual degree of risk.[27]

Expanded Criminalization

Both federal and state laws exist that have criminalized some forms of particularly egregious speech. The crafting of these laws always requires a balancing of free speech protections against the harm caused by egregious speech. These laws have been modified in virtually all states and at the national level to specifically address speech that is transmitted in electronic form. This is a sound response.

The efforts that present concerns are the attempts to expand the criminal laws to encompass greater kinds of speech, when such speech is transmitted online. The first effort in this regard was the ill-fated Computer Decency Act which sought to criminalize the online distribution of materials that were materials that were "obscene or indecent" to persons known to be under 18. This Act, enacted in 1996 was held unconstitutional by the U.S. Supreme Court in 1997.

The current embodiment of the "expanded criminalization" effort is H 6123, Megan Meier Cyberbullying Prevention Act, which would impose criminal penalties on a range of online speech. Numerous legal authorities have indicated that this proposed statute would violate principles of free speech.[28] Leading researchers and professionals in the field of cyberbullying have also raised concerns about this approach.[29]

Encourage Use of Parental Control/Filtering Technologies to Restrict or Monitor Teens

Parental control technologies include technologies that parents or others can use to seek to limit the access of young people to objectionable material online, establish time limits, and monitor online activities. Frequently, guidance to parents encourages the use of these technologies. The Children's

---

23 Wolak, J., Finkelhor, D., Mitchell, K., & Ybarra, M. (2008) Online "Predators" and their Victims: Myths, Realities and Implications for Prevention and Treatment. *American Psychologist*, 63, 111-128. http://www.unh.edu/ccrc/internet-crimes/papers.html.

24 Lenhart, A., Madden, M., Rankin, A., & Smith, A., (2007) *Teens and Social Media: The use of social media gains a greater foothold in teen life as email continues to lose its luster.* Pew Internet & American Life Project. http://www.pewinternet.org/PPF/r/230/report_display.asp.

25 Kim, K., Ryu, E. Chon, M., Yeun, E., Choi, S.,, Seo, J., Nam, B. (2006) Internet addiction in Korean adolescents and its relation to depression and suicidal ideation: A questionnaire survey International. *Journal of Nursing Studies*, 43, 185–192. (The levels of depression and suicide ideation were highest in the internet-addicts group.); Jenaro, C., Flores, N., Mez-vela, M., Gonza, F., Gil, L., Caballo, C. (2007) Problematic internet and cell-phone use: Psychological, behavioral, and health correlates, *Addiction Research and Theory*. 15(3): 309–320 (Heavy internet use is associated with high anxiety; high cell-phone use is associated to being female, and having high anxiety and insomnia.)

26 Block, J.J. (2008) Issues for DSM-V: Internet Addiction, *Am J Psychiatry* 165:306-307, doi: 10.1176/appi.ajp.2007.07101556, http://ajp.psychiatryonline.org/cgi/content/full/165/3/306.

27 Roush, W. (2006) The Moral Panic Over Social Networking Sites. *Technology Review*. http://www.technologyreview.com/communications/17266/?a=f. See also, Cohen, S. (1972). *Folk devils and moral panics: the creation of the Mods and Rockers*. London: MacGibbon and Kee.

28 Kotler, S. (May 14, 2009) Cyberbullying Bill Could Ensnare Free Speech Rights. Fox News. http://www.foxnews.com/politics/2009/05/14/cyberbullying-ensnare-free-speech-rights/.

29 Statement presented to House Judiciary Subcommittee on Crime, Terrorism, and Homeland Security on September 30, 2009

Internet Protection Act (2000) requires schools and libraries that receive federal funds for technology, including the E-Rate, to use technology protection measure (filtering) to block access to visual images that are obscene, child pornography, or harmful to minors.[30]

The use parental control technologies by parents of younger children can be effective. Several companies, including Symantec and Microsoft have recently introduced effective family safety technologies. Filtering software can be used effectively in elementary schools, although it will not prevent all instances of accidental access.

As an alternative to filtering, parents are now encouraged to install monitoring software. This approach is guaranteed to undermine the quality of a parent-child relationship and lead teens to find ways to use the Internet that circumvent such monitoring. The use of monitoring of Internet traffic in schools, if part of a comprehensive management program, can be more effective. However, if students are inclined to engage in misuse, they will simply do so using their own personal digital devices.

A little understood challenge to the reliance on parental control/filtering technologies is grounded in the work of other federal agencies, including the Broadcasting Board of Governors (BBG) which manages all U.S. civilian international broadcasting including Voice of America, which have sought to ensure the availability of technologies to bypass the filters and monitoring by countries in Asia and the Middle East where access to the Internet is highly censored.[31] Conducting a search on the terms "bypass Internet filters" will yield an impressive number of sites that provide guidance on the use of these bypass technologies.

Senator Spector recently published a commentary addressing this issue.[32] In *Attack the Cyberwalls!: The Internet is the Pathway to Democracy in Places Like Iran*, he advocated significantly expanded research efforts to develop technologies that will allow for both bypassing and anonymity for citizens in countries with repressive regimes. "The walls used by 21st century tyrannies to isolate and control their citizens are increasingly electronic rather than physical barriers. American interests and values will be powerfully advanced in finding ways to breach those walls."

It appears that teens were generally unaware of these bypass technologies until the exploding popularity of the social networking sites. At this point in time, most high school students know, or know someone who knows, how to bypass the filter. The only people in schools who are blocked from accessing sites by the filter are the adult staff. Bottom line: it is not possible, nor developmentally appropriate, to keep teens in electronically fenced play yards.

Inaccurate Fear-Based Messaging - Reefer Madness and "Just say 'No'" Revisited

Much of the currently available Internet safety curriculum for students and presentations for parents was developed by organizations funded by the U.S. Department of Justice or has been created or funded by state law enforcement officials associated with the Internet Crimes Against Children task forces or the state attorneys general. Most of this curriculum presents inaccurate, fear-based information and simplistic "just say 'no'" rules that advocate against normative online behavior, delivered by adults in an authoritarian manner. The most common Internet safety messages - and the concerns associated with these messages - include:

- "Don't post personal information or pictures." This message is conveys the mistaken perception that posting information will allow predators to track and abduct teens. Posting information about yourself and pictures in protected social networking profiles, sharing more general information in public environments, and providing personal contact information during registration or for purchasing is normative online behavior. The degree of risk depends on the type of information or images posted and place such information is shared.
- "Don't talk to online strangers." I-Safe, an Internet safety organization that has received millions in federal funds through the Department of Justice tells middle school students that if they communicate with online strangers, they are "willing participants" in online predation. Children are regularly

30 http://www.fcc.gov/ogb/consumerfacts/cipa.html

31 Peacefire/Voice of America 2003 http://sethf.com/infothought/blog/archives/000167.html. Peacefire has joined forces with Voice of America <http://www.ibb.gov/>, a federal agency that used to do pro-democracy radio broadcasts into communist Eastern Europe and Asia, and is currently still broadcasting into China while branching out into finding ways to defeat Internet censorship. They've contracted with us to help defeat the "Great Firewall of China", the firewalls put in place by the Chinese censors to block people in China from reading foreign Web sites that criticize the Chinese government. The technology could be extended to help people in other regions such as the Middle East where the Internet is heavily censored.

32 7/2009. http://www.huffingtonpost.com/sen-arlen-specter/attack-the-cyberwalls-the_b_227114.html

communicating with strangers in safe children's sites like Club Penguin and Webkinz. Stranger danger warnings are known to be entirely ineffective. Young people face far greater risks online in harmful interactions with known peers. They face far greater risks of sexual abuse by family members and acquaintances.

- "If something makes you uncomfortable online, tell an adult." Given that young people know that adults are not as comfortable with digital technologies and environments as they are and that adults are regularly trying to inculcate fear about the digital environments where they feel safe and intend to engage in safe and responsible behavior, there is little mystery as to why young people are routinely ignoring this guidance.

Following the online sexual predator technopanic, has been the inaccurately reported story of the unfortunate suicide of Megan Meiers.[33] Of significant concern is the media reporting and use by some Internet safety advocates of this incident that has been contrary to the recommendations for media on reporting on suicide enunciated by this nation's leading authorities on suicide prevention.[34] Specifically these guidelines state: "The cause of an individual suicide is invariably more complicated than a recent painful event such as the break-up of a relationship or the loss of a job." "Dramatizing the impact of suicide through descriptions and pictures of grieving relatives, teachers or classmates or community expressions of grief may encourage potential victims to see suicide as a way of getting attention or as a form of retaliation against others." It is essential to stop trying to encourage Internet safety by communicating that suicide is an option for youth to consider.

Subsequent to the publication of the research findings of the Berkman Task Force, the fear-based messaging about online sexual predators and simplistic safety rules associated with these concerns appear to be disappearing. The Federal Trade Commission's OnGuard Online web site represents an excellent example of effective educational messaging.[35]

Many curriculum producers have created or will soon be introducing instructional materials addressing digital media safety and literacy that presents material that is accurate and grounded in effective risk prevention. These organizations, which have not relied on federal funding, include CyberSmart, Common Sense Media, and Center for Safe and Responsible Internet Use.

Recommendations for Action

21st Century Learning Environment

The necessary foundation to address digital media safety and literacy

It is imperative that our nation's schools establish 21st Century learning environment, enriched with interactive Web 2.0 technologies, including blogs, wikis, pod/video casting, interest networks. Such environments are essential to prepare students for their future education, career, civic responsibilities, and personal life. It is impossible to prepare students for their future in classrooms designed to serve our past! 21st Century skills are necessary to maintain U.S. effectiveness and competitiveness in the global community. Such environment is also essential to teach digital media safety and literacy (DMSL).

The current barriers to the creation of 21st Century learning environment include:

- The standardization of 20th Century curriculum and instruction grounded in high stakes testing. The current manner in which school success is measured removes the time and incentive to make the changes necessary to embrace the future. Teachers lack the professional expertise to effectively

---

33 Contrary to the information widely reported, Lori Drew did not come up with the idea of creating the profile, did not create the profile, and did not send or direct any messages, including the last nasty ones. The news coverage did not address concerns associated with the fact that a 13 year old emotionally vulnerable girl was allowed to develop an online romantic relationship with a 16 year boy who no one knew in person and who did not even have a telephone. http://suburbanjournals.stltoday.com/articles/2007/11/13/news/sj2tn20071110-1111stc_pokin_1.ii1.tx; http://suburbanjournals.stltoday.com/articles/2007/12/03/news/doc47543edb763a7031547461.txt; http://www.wired.com/threatlevel/2008/11/lori-drew-pla-3/

34 http://www.sprc.org/library/sreporting.pdf. Reporting on Suicide: Recommendations for the Media, Centers for Disease Control and Prevention, National Institute of Mental Health, Office of the Surgeon General Substance Abuse and Mental Health Services Administration, American Foundation for Suicide Prevention, American Association of Suicidology, Annenberg Public Policy Center

35 http://www.onguardonline.gov/.

integrate Web 2.0-based interactions into their curriculum and instruction. A new vision for school and student success is needed.

- Overreliance on filtering to manage student Internet use. The filters are blocking highly relevant instructional material. High school students are easily able to bypass the filter. School staff are frequently not granted the authority to override the filter to access material for instructional use and, even more concerning, often safe school personnel are not able to override the filter to investigate online material posted by students upon report of concerns to student safety and well-being. Filtering is a Web 1.0 protection tool that merely blocks access to objectionable material. Filtering is ineffective in managing interactive communications. New approaches to management are necessary.
- The irresponsible fear-based statements made about social networking have lead educational leaders to be concerned about a negative reaction of parents and the community if they integrate these technologies into the learning environment.
- There are legitimate concerns about potential liability of school districts related to publishing torts and copyright infringement associated with student and staff posting material online. In the 1990's, Internet service providers and institutions of higher education were provided by federal statute with limited liability if they established policies and abuse reporting and take-down procedures. It was not contemplated at that time that K-12 students or teachers would even post material online. This barrier can be easily removed through federal legislation.

Recommended Legislative Strategies

- In reauthorization of Elementary and Secondary Education Act, remove barriers to 21st Century learning, ensure technology plans address use of web 2.0 technologies and provide adequate funds for professional/curriculum development supporting 21st Century learning.
- Enact federal legislation to provide K-12 schools with limited liability for student/staff postings that may constitute copyright infringement or be a publishing tort. Require policy, abuse report, and take-down.

Universal Digital Media Safety and Literacy Education (DMSL)

The objective of providing universal digital media safety and literacy education is that all young people will: Understand risks and protective strategies and engage in safe behavior. Demonstrate respect for others. Take responsibility for the well-being of others. Because the majority of young people are generally making good choices online it is possible to use social norms/peer leadership instructional strategies. This approach to risk prevention has demonstrated a high degree of effectiveness.

Instructional opportunities that are present in schools include: Direct instruction in appropriate classes, including library, technology, health classes. Informal education through the use of signage and material displayed during log-in on the computer screens. Infused throughout Web 2.0 curriculum. "Teachable moments," including incidents and news stories that provide the opportunity for discussion and reflection.

Schools also need to educate parents. This can be accomplished through parent workshops, information sent home in school news letters, and "just in time" resources in the school library or counselor's office.

The current challenges to the delivery of effective digital media safety and literacy curriculum include:

- "Legacy" curriculum, funded or created by law enforcement. This curriculum is not grounded in effective risk prevention. It contains inaccurate information, uses fear-based messages, presents simplistic rules, and is designed to be delivered in authoritarian manner. Fortunately, more effective curriculum is coming onto the market.
- Lack of teacher understanding of digital media safety and literacy issues. There is an need for extensive professional development.
- As noted in the prior section, the demands on schools ties to high stakes testing has removed the time and incentive to shift to 21st Century learning. This also makes it difficult to support the addition of new curriculum.
- The current financial pressures on schools are causing overall challenges, but also leading to loss of library media specialists, whose involvement is critical because of their expertise in media literacy.

The Protecting Children in the 21st Century Act, part of the Broadband Data Improvement Act adds a requirement to the Children's Internet Protection Act. This new requirement reads: "(iii) as part of its

Internet safety policy is educating minors about appropriate online behavior, including interacting with other individuals on social networking websites and in chat rooms and cyberbullying awareness and response." The regulations for this new requirement have not yet been announced.[36] In the existing regulations for CIPA, the FCC maintained a perspective that school districts should be respected to act in good faith in regards to Internet safety and the implementation of CIPA. Because the new statute requires changes to the Internet safety policy, it is reasonable to presume that changes will need to be made to district policy and that such changes will require a board hearing.

The major opportunity presented by this new requirement is the incentive provided to districts to engage in planning regarding how all aspects of digital media safety and literacy can be effectively integrated into the curriculum. Districts should be encouraged to use this new requirement to expand discussions on how these issues can be effectively integrated into the curriculum.

Recommended Strategies

- In reauthorization of ESEA:
  - Require State and Local Education Agencies to develop plan for digital media safety and literacy instruction. Ensure the involvement of library media, educational technology, and safe school personnel in this development.
  - Expand the use of library media specialists as facilitating teachers for digital media safety and literacy instruction. Library media specialists have the greatest background in the foundational aspects of 21st Century learning. Their role will be critical to the success of schools in making the shift to this new instruction.
  - Provide discretionary grants for State and Local Education Agencies for innovative digital media safety and literacy instruction activities.
- It is not recommended that federal government fund the development of digital media safety and literacy curriculum. This is best accomplished by private sector.

Targeted Youth Risk Online Prevention & Intervention

Young people at greatest risk online are those at greater risk offline. They have psychosocial problems, engage in risk behavior, and have disrupted relationships with parents. But young people without significant risk factors also engage in risky online behavior. Online risk behavior could result in criminal victimization or behavior. It often will result in disruptive impact at school.

It is essential to address youth risk online in collaborative, multidisciplinary manner - involving education (safe schools, educational technology, library media), law enforcement (juvenile justice and Internet crimes), and community mental health.

It must be recognized that the traditional manner in which risk prevention initiatives are implemented will not be effective in addressing these concerns. Risk prevention initiatives are required to implement evidence-based best practices. This requirement is grounded in very excellent motives - to ensure that funds are expended for prevention and intervention approaches that have demonstrated effectiveness. The process by which programs are developed and evaluated is long and complicated.

Unfortunately, this approach will not work to address the new risks presented by digital media. The research in this area is still emerging, thus the essential foundation for development of prevention and intervention initiatives is not yet fully understood. There are no evidence-based best practices. Given the time it generally takes to establish that a practice has demonstrated effectiveness, a program that sought to obtain such status would be obsolete even before such status could be obtained, because the technologies and digital activities are changing so rapidly.

To address the concerns of youth risk online it simply will not be possible to emulate traditional risk prevention initiatives that fund relatively static programs using evidence-based best practices. It is necessary to shift to a continuous improvement model. Fortunately, there is already statutory guidance on how to accomplish this. Under the current Safe and Drug Free Schools and Communities Act, requirement have been established to allow schools and organizations to obtain to obtain a waiver of the

---

36 This statute makes an amendment to CIPA. The following is information about the existing CIPA requirements http://www.fcc.gov/cgb/consumerfacts/cipa.html

requirement that programs are evidence-based.[37] The excellent requirements to achieve such a waiver can provide the necessary foundation to ensure that programs to address youth risk online will have a strong likelihood of success. The requirements include:

- A needs assessment based on objective data that describes the problems or concerns currently faced.
- A detailed description of the implementation plan, including performance measures program activities, personnel, audience, timeline, and costs.
- The rationale for the activity including how it is designed and why it is expected to be successful, the risk and protective factors the program is designed to address, and evidence to support that the program has a "likelihood of success." This evidence must identify the current youth risk online research insight and effective prevention approaches that have been incorporated into the activity.
- An evaluation plan that addresses the methods used to assess progress and how results of the evaluation and new research insight will be used to refine, improve, and strengthen the comprehensive plan.

The current challenges that must be addressed to proceed effectively to address youth risk online include:

- The mental health and health professional and research community currently have a significant lack of understanding of youth risk online issues and the digital culture. As noted, there is a lack of sufficient research, no evidence-based best practices, and rapidly changing technologies and online activities. Thus the typical manner in which risk prevention professionals respond to challenges cannot be followed.
- There is the lack of vehicle to provide ongoing assessment of online risk behavior, risk factors, and protective factors, that can be used to measure effectiveness of interventions. Currently, the Center for Disease Control conducts a biannual Youth Risk Behavior Survey.[38] This survey provides excellent insight into the types and incident rates of risky behavior, risk factors, and protective factors. The survey results allow for the evaluation of prevention and intervention initiatives. This survey is designed to be administered in one class period. Competition is intense to add any new questions. It is essential to more effectively obtain survey data on youth risk online concerns, incident rates, risk and protective factors - and to compare this data with the data on the Youth Risk Behavior Survey.
- President Obama's proposed budget has eliminated funding for State and Local Education Agency safe school programs (Title IV). This program is undergoing revision to focus more strongly on the creation of positive school climates However, the elimination of this state and local infrastructure - at this critical juncture - will seriously undermine all efforts to effectively address youth risk online. The staff who are funded at the state and local level to coordinate safe schools issues must be in the position to coordinate the activities to address these new concerns to the safety and well-being of students. While some of the legacy safe schools and drug prevention programs may be eliminated, it is imperative that this delivery infrastructure remain viable.

Recommended Strategies

- Sufficient funding to accomplish to maintain the state and local safe schools infrastructure must be appropriated to allow for initiation of state and local efforts to address these new concerns.
- In reauthorization of ESEA, Title IV, require State and Local Education Agencies to develop comprehensive plans to address youth risk online. These plans should be develop in collaboration with law enforcement and mental health.
- Establish discretionary grant program emulating multidisciplinary approach taken in Safe Schools/ Healthy Students program, which involves Substance Abuse and Mental Health Division, Department of Education, and Office of Juvenile Justice and Delinquency Prevention. Provide support for:
  - Mental health programs (SAMHSA), programs addressing criminal victimization/behavior (OJJPD), school programs (DOE).
  - National, state, and community programs, including online programs and professional development.

---

37 Section 4115. http://www.ed.gov/policy/elsec/leg/esea02/pg52.html.

38 http://www.cdc.gov/HealthyYouth/yrbs/index.htm.

- Ensure innovation under conditions that require accurate statement of problem, coherent approach, and ongoing evaluation to meet the requirements of a waiver of the Principles of Effectiveness.

- Direct the Center for Disease Control to conduct a Youth Risk Behavior Online Survey as companion to Youth Risk Behavior Survey.

Mr. SCOTT. Thank you.

Professor Palfrey?

TESTIMONY OF JOHN PALFREY, LAW PROFESSOR, HARVARD LAW SCHOOL, CAMBRIDGE, MA

Mr. Palfrey. Mr. Chairman, thank you so very much for the honor of the invitation to be here. Ranking Member Gohmert and Members of the Subcommittee, thank you for focusing attention on this important issue. I want to speak first to the research that has been done in this area and then speak to a few of the solutions discussed today.

I think that, Mr. Chairman, you described the state of the research extremely well. I have spent the last few years in the field doing research myself, talking to kids, parents, teachers, social workers, and others, but also, as the Chair of the Internet Safety Technical Task Force, which was commissioned by the Attorneys General, reviewed much of the research done by others in this field.

I think that the state of affairs is that bullying online is on the rise. No matter how you define it, no serious observer disputes that fact. I think that one of the key aspects of this is that what we are seeing is that public spaces have moved from playgrounds to online spaces, online spaces often owned by private companies and online spaces that are often highly distributed.

So, as we think about this, I think we need to think about, how do we want to govern behavior in these online spaces, and noting that kids don't distinguish between their online lives and offline lives; it is mostly just life. So it urged us, in thinking about this, to focus less on the cyber part of cyberbullying and think of it as bullying, which is, I think, how most kids do.

I think part of the problem, too, is this gulf that many have acknowledged between parents and teachers, social workers, and others who don't feel that they have the tools to help, and the kids themselves who are engaging in risky behaviors in these online spaces, just as they do in the offline. And I think that any solution that we look at needs to address this problem of the gulf to put the right tools in the hands of parents, teachers, social workers, pediatricians, and others who are touching our kids' lives.

Turning to potential solutions, I think the Committee has done a great job at identifying potentials in this area. I think no one disputes the notion that this will require a series of different solutions, a series of different solutions with education at the core. I think it also goes without saying that parents have the greatest obligation here, and kids themselves. This is something that is most sensibly dealt with in the home.

But I think we should also look to opportunities like using technologies as part of the solution and working with companies who are, in a way, the overseers of these playgrounds in many respects, and, of course, looking to the law.

I would share the view that criminalization is not the answer, with due respect to Ms. Sánchez. I won't go into that since others have touched on the constitutionality, but also the effectiveness of that. I think it is crucial that law enforcement play a role in this space, but it needs to be, I think, a backstop.

I think the education support described in the "AWARE Act" is precisely the right place to start from here. I think that, in reading the "AWARE Act," one thing it does very well is to track the research in the field. It talks about public and private-type partnerships. It looks at at-risk kids, where we know many of the problems are.

And I think it has been drafted in such a way as to support those kinds of activities that need supporting. And, as someone working in this field, I am keenly aware of the fact that there is not sufficient support for exactly this kind of work and that it is the most promising, even though even that will not get the entire job done.

I would point to one other potential approach that, Mr. Chairman, you mentioned, about revisiting section 230 of the "Communications Decency Act." I say this with some trepidation. There are many I respect who think this is a terrible idea, what I am about to say, and these are smart people.

There is a statute on the books that exempts from liability online intermediaries, and that has been a very important part, I think, over the last decade or so of Federal legislation in this area. It has allowed for a great deal of innovation and so forth.

But I do think that there are instances where this immunity is broad enough that bad actors are able to hide behind it in a way that disincentivizes the "good samaritan" behavior that you in the Congress thought about when you were passing this statute.

Again, I would urge great caution in tinkering with this statute. Again, the costs, the demerits of this are with respect to innovation, and they might be very great in some cases. But I think we need to make sure that the law overall is incentivizing the kind of behaviors that we see in many good companies, Facebook and other social networks, that really exemplify good behavior here, while disallowing the bad actors from hiding behind a shield that we didn't mean to give them. So I would urge a look in that direction.

But, again, no one approach is going to solve the problem. I think that the community-based approaches that have been discussed today are precisely the right angle. And, again, I commend the Committee for focusing attention on this important issue.

Thank you.

[The prepared statement of Mr. Palfrey follows:]

PREPARED STATEMENT OF JOHN PALFREY

Hearing on Cyberbullying and other Online Safety Issues for Children; H.R. 1966, the "Megan Meier Cyberbullying Prevention Act"; and H.R. 3630, the "Adolescent Web Awareness Requires Education Act (AWARE Act)"

Committee on the Judiciary
Subcommittee on Crime, Terrorism, and Homeland Security

Testimony of John Palfrey, Harvard Law School

September 30, 2009

Thank you, Mr. Chairman, and members of the Subcommittee on Crime, Terrorism, and Homeland Security. Through this hearing and your work to advance legislation, you are focusing public attention on an important issue: the extent to which our young people, and adults, are harming one another in online spaces. Cyberbullying is a complex and growing problem. Your leadership is greatly appreciated. Together, there is much that we can do, especially on behalf of America's young people, to keep them safer online, from this and other threats to their health and well-being.

Problem.

By virtually all accounts, bullying of young people by their peers online is on the rise. The magnitude of this increase depends heavily on how one defines the term "bullying," exactly. Results of recent studies vary widely in this respect. The harm caused to young people by their peers, and by adults, primarily psychological in nature, can be substantial. Sometimes the harm falls in the category of teasing that few would say we should regulate; sometimes, the actions are so harmful in nature that they already violate civil or criminal law. And unfortunately, in the worst cases, bullying properly falls on the spectrum of physical and sexual abuse. No serious observer disputes that we are observing a significant increase in bullying online.

The topic of cyberbullying caught the attention of the members of the Internet Safety Technical Task Force last year, which I chaired. The Task Force brought together representatives of twenty-nine leading companies, child advocacy groups, and academics. We worked together throughout 2008 to analyze the safety issues facing young people online. We began, as the Attorneys General who commissioned the study requested, looking at the problems of unwanted contact and access to harmful content online.

In the process of researching the risks to children online, concern about bullying kept arising as a key concern. The final report of the Task Force included an extensive literature review, drafted by the scholars danah boyd and Andrew Schrock and supported by a blue-ribbon academic advisory board. While sexual predation and unwanted content continue to be substantial concerns which merit our attention, the dramatic rise in recent years has been the increase in the likelihood that children will suffer harm online at the hands of their peers. (See http://cyber.law.harvard.edu/pubrelease/isttf/)

The data that show a sharp increase in bullying online need to be considered in light of a series of additional bits of context. First, overwhelmingly, most of the ways in which young people use digital technologies is positive. (See, for instance, the work of Mimi Ito et al. at http://digitalyouth.ischool.berkeley.edu/report) These technologies have become part of the fabric of the life of young people. Most young people, at least in the United States, do not distinguish between their "online" and "offline" lives. As a result, many of the good things that have gone on offline also happen, in one form or another, online; so, too, do many of the bad things that happen in everyday life play out also online.

Second, it's an open question among researchers as to whether bullying overall is on the rise or not. Again, it is quite clear that more young people are bullying one another than ever before via digital technologies. What is not clear is whether this replaces any traditional, offline forms of bullying. It could be that bullying is neither up nor down as an overall trend, but rather just shifting venues – and coming to our attention more prominently as a result. It also may be that bullying is all of a sudden brought to the attention of adults who previously could not see it happening on the playground or in the schoolyard. It may be, too, that bullying is, for the first time, recorded for adults and others to see after the fact. That does not change the very real harm caused to individual young people by bullying online, but it does mean that we should be cautious before we call this bullying an epidemic.

As a side note, worth pausing on briefly: It's also the case that sometimes adults are part of the problem, not part of the solution. Adults are often involved in bullying youth – or other adults – online. Adults are, too rarely, part of the solution in terms of modeling good behavior and helping to support young people who are seeking to do the right thing.

The third important thing is to focus on the behavior – how people use digital media – and not solely on the technology. Digital technologies themselves do not have a "nature." The Internet, as one core part of the digital architecture, is famously a "stupid" network. A key design principle of the Internet, the end-to-end principle, calls for it to "pass all packets." The network, and the applications that are built upon it, is not inherently "good" or "bad"; it is merely a conduit for human and machine-to-machine interaction. A related point: technology design, or architecture, can affect behavior. As we consider solutions, we should pay close attention to the fact that both technological design and changes in how people are likely to behave can be drivers of solutions.

No single solution to cyberbullying – or, more properly, bullying in general – exists. There is no one thing that we can do that will protect America's young people from being harmed online. The behavior that we would like to curtail – most commonly, young people saying or doing harmful things to other young people online – is part of typical adolescent behavior to some extent. In many cases, what concerns us is behavior that we want to stop, but not to criminalize; the image of filling our prisons with teenagers and young adults who have been teasing one another online is plainly unattractive. And many of the more aggressive responses to online bullying would curtail First Amendment freedoms that minors ought to enjoy as their parents and teachers do. All the same, it's too great a worry to make throwing up our hands an adequate response.

Solutions.

The most effective solution to cyberbullying is to combine a series of approaches to protect minors. This notion is true of the vast majority of problems online; there is rarely a single approach that will satisfactorily solve the problem. Education, technology, and law reform each have a role to play.

The first place to look is to the young people themselves. Minors can help address the problem because they can lead by example. Young people listen to one another, and together they establish powerful social norms. This is particularly true in terms how young people act in the context of online social environments. Constructive social norms can lead to widespread change in how young people act in online environments; likewise, social norms (such as a willingness to download music illegally) can lead to widespread lawbreaking.

Education is crucial. Parents, teachers, and other adult mentors need to intervene with the young people in their lives, to give guidance about how to interact with one another and to lead by example. Parents and teachers can, in the course of conversation, shed light on the potential harm that online bullying can cause and the consequences for both the bully and the person who is being harmed. Other young people – say, college students returning to their high school for a community meeting – might help to spark these important conversations within schools and after-school environments. It is possible to make certain harmful behavior "uncool" in such a way as to reduce the incidence of young people hurting one another in these ways.

Technology companies can help, too. The large social networks that youth frequent – Facebook, MySpace, MyYearbook, BlackPlanet, LiveJournal, Bebo, and so forth – can help to set a tone for behavior that is permissible and that which is not. Communities can be given tools to self-police and rules on the site can ban harmful speech. By contrast, some online web sites – the AutoAdmit message board for admitted law students leaps to mind, as does the now-defunct JuicyCampus – too often support a very negative, often nasty sort of online discourse.

New law.

In light of the growing likelihood of harm occurring to young people at the hands of online bullies, our instinct to regulate the digital environment through law more aggressively makes perfect sense. As parents and teachers, we find ourselves at a loss to stop harm that is happening to their children and students. School administrators worry that their policies are out of date. Law enforcement officials puzzle over when and whether they have a role in helping young people in these circumstances.

New legislation could help to address cyberbullying and other online safety problems. But newly criminalizing a broad swath of online speech is not the right general approach. Nor do I favor a set of rules that apply only in cyberspace and not in offline life. The rules should, to the greatest extent possible, be the same in the online context as offline. We should strive to apply rules of general applicability to the Internet context. Where the facts change – as in the realm of Internet safety – we ought to rethink the way we write and apply these general rules, to be sure.

In many respects, the law already helps to provide causes of action against cyberbullies. If online speech involved is defamatory, the bully (whether an adult or a young person) may be found directly liable for harm done to her peer. If the speech is obscene, if it rises to the level of a true threat, or if it is intimidating, the act of posting it online might violate a host of civil and criminal laws. The issue in these cases is enforcement, not whether or not the speech is unlawful in the first place.

There are legal approaches – other than newly criminalizing online speech – that make sense.

The "Adolescent Web Awareness Requires Education Act of 2009" is a terrific proposal. The Act's proposed grant program would make a great deal of difference for young people in the near term and potentially in the long term. The priorities stated in the bill track effectively the research about young people and their risky behaviors. It emphasizes at-risk youth. It calls for partnerships between the private and public sectors. It calls for close connection between the research community and those in our schools and communities.

Some of the innovation that we ought to explore involves the use of technology within online communities to provide support for young people in these contexts. We ought to develop, refine, and implement curricular approaches to cyberbullying. We need to provide training to parents, teachers, administrators, and other staff in schools and other environments where young people spend time. The terrific network of social workers and pediatricians and other professionals who support children need to be part of the solution, too. And we need to put tools in the hands of the young people who are helping one another address this problem by investing in peer-driven solutions. This grant program could help creative people to build this infrastructure.

Rethinking existing law.

Just as we consider new legislation, we ought to consider changes to existing laws to address this safety concern among children. In particular, we need to re-examine existing law with a view toward enforceability, which tends to be the biggest problem with cyberlaws in general, and toward ensuring that our core principles and desired outcomes are accomplished by laws that were written for an analog-only age. Where law enforcement officers don't have the tools they need, in law or in budget, we need to address these shortfalls. But the answer is not to create a layer of new, cyber-specific rules on top of the existing legal regime that governs any particular area of activity.

One law that ought to be reconsidered in light of youth safety online is the Communications Decency Act Section 230, part of the Telecommunications Act of 1996. CDA 230 is a cornerstone of the legal framework that has enabled the information technology sector to thrive over the past decade. It has also had a crucial part in ensuring that the Internet has become a place where free expression, like innovation, also thrives. Both economic growth (promoted through technological innovation) and free expression are much to be celebrated and supported through careful policymaking. Those who drafted and fought to sustain CDA 230 deserve our thanks.

But it is time to re-examine how far CDA 230's immunity extends. A lot has happened over the past decade. Those who drafted this provision would have had a hard time anticipating the changes that have ensued – and quite how broadly this immunity would extend over time. To be clear, courts that have extended the immunity fairly broadly (the general posture of most courts that have taken up cases at the edges of this area of doctrine) have been right – on the law as it stands – to do so. The law, as written, shields from liability MySpace, for instance, in the Julie Doe case in Texas, or Craigslist in the cases associated with Section 8 housing, and so forth.

In my view, these types of cases are not rightly decided, though, from the perspective of what the law ought to protect or not to protect.

In the context of online safety, the law needs to provide an incentive for technology companies to do the right thing. The law should avoid establishing a framework that allows technology companies to ignore the problems that their young users are encountering online. Take the hypothetical case of a young person who is physically harmed after meeting someone in an online environment. The young person (or his parents, more likely) seeks to bring suit against the service provider involved. In my view, the service provider should not have special protection from such a tort claim. Such a claim should be decided on the merits. Was the service provider negligent? Or not? The fact that the service provider is offering an Internet-based service, rather than a physically-based service, should result in an automatic shield to liability.

Most major social networks in the United States would not likely be liable for the harm in such terrible instances. The most prominent social networks, like Facebook and MySpace, are taking more and more affirmative steps to make their online environments safer for kids – such that a negligence claim ought not reach them. But the claim should not be barred at the courthouse door, in my view. The opposite incentive should be at work: to encourage them to continue their innovation to protect kids.

The Congress ought to consider how to ensure that online intermediaries have an obligation not to ignore harm that is occurring to their users online. Online gossip sites like AutoAdmit and Juicy Campus have become symbols of bad behavior because the site operators often refuse to cooperate with victims to help those who were harmed by defamation on their site. Many students, among others, are bullied – presumably by peers who knew them – through defamatory online expression on these online forums. For quite some time, the students harmed had no recourse: the site operators refused to take down the harmful material, even when notified of the harm, and the students could not identify the people who had posted the harmful speech anonymously because the site operators claimed not to keep any log files. The site operators hid behind federal law: Section 230 of the Communications Decency Act, which provided them a safe harbor.

The growth of online bullying and other online safety risks means it is time to rethink this particular safe harbor in terms of its breadth. The question to ask is whether such site operators might have some form of affirmative obligation in cases where harm to minors is clear. One could imagine at least two ways to amend the safe harbor. The lighter-touch approach would be to require intermediaries to retain log files for a certain period of time and to participate in law enforcement efforts to bring those who defame others to justice. Alternately, one could require online intermediaries to respond to notice from those who have been defamed by taking down the defamatory content if the intermediary wishes to be protected by the safe harbor (which is what we do in the context of copyright, through Section 512 of the Digital Millennium Copyright Act). A third approach could be to exempt intermediaries from the safe harbor of CDA 230 altogether in cases where there has been harm to young people as a result of harmful speech, a carve-out that parallels the carve-out in CDA 230 for copyright complaints.

Each of these changes to the law would have demerits. Critics of such tinkering with Section 230 point – correctly – to the risks to innovation online that such changes to the liability regime might give rise. To establish a notice and take-down procedure to track to the copyright processes would no doubt have a chilling effect on some speech online and it would add to transaction costs associated with running an online intermediary which presently do not exist. A requirement to retain log files would have a negative effect on individual privacy in an era where privacy interests are already under attack. But these demerits are outweighed by the need to address present, and potentially growing, risks to young people online.

Conclusion.

There is no easy answer to the problem of online bullying. The most effective approach – education, with a view toward getting toward the root cause of bullying and establishing positive social norms – is the hardest to accomplish. It is also the least satisfying as an answer. The AWARE Act is a good step in the right direction. We should consider other approaches, including law reform and the use of new technologies in online environments, but we should do so in the knowledge that these approaches are likely half-measures at best – partial solutions to this growing problem facing our kids and our society at large.

Mr. SCOTT. Thank you, Professor Palfrey.

We will now recognize ourselves under the 5-minute rule to ask questions.

I will begin with Professor O'Neil. You used an interesting term involving the Constitution, "promising." That didn't quite get us there. I assume there would be no problems if the communications involved threats.

Mr. O'NEIL. That certainly is a recognized exception. The Supreme Court has never really defined "true threat." They have used that phrase and implied that true threats are not constitutionally protected, like fraud and inducement and accessory before the fact and a whole other range of uses of language that are not protected speech.

My assumption is that, and I think that both of you pointed to this possibility, some elements in a cyberbullying communication or a series of cyberbullying messages undoubtedly would be threats, but I would think the greater part of the kind of cyberbullying message that creates the greatest concern, indeed anguish, among those who seek to redress are not really threats. They aren't incitement, they aren't fighting words, they aren't libel. They don't fit into any of these categories.

Mr. SCOTT. You suggested that intentional affliction of emotional distress is normally a civil action, not criminal.

Mr. O'NEIL. It is.

Mr. SCOTT. Can you convert it into a crime?

Mr. O'NEIL. It has not been done, to my knowledge.

Mr. SCOTT. Is it protected from criminal, but not protected from civil?

Mr. O'NEIL. It is so clearly—the classic case being one person as a cruel joke or a hoax sends an e-mail message to somebody else saying, so sorry to hear of your brother's death last week, when, in fact, the brother is alive and well. It has been widely assumed—I have never seen a first amendment jurisprudence or scholarship to the contrary—that in a classic situation of that kind, a civil recovery would be feasible. The Falwell-Hustler case to which Mr. Silverglate referred is in some ways troublesome, but the Supreme Court's concern was that Reverend Falwell was a very prominent public figure, and as a public figure plaintiff, by analogy to the New York Times privilege, he was denied recovery.

Mr. SCOTT. We don't have that public figure exception in criminal law, do we?

Mr. O'NEIL. Probably not, although the context of which we are talking, cyberbullying, almost inevitably involves people who are not public figures. And until it becomes a media issue, for example, or leads to litigation, they are neither public figures, nor are they engaged in a matter of public concerns. So I am assuming we passed that barrier.

But as I noted in my prepared testimony, the absence really of any either supportive or preclusive reasoning with respect to a criminal application of intentional infliction of emotional distress is an issue. I just am not aware of any jurisprudence or scholarship that argues strongly either way. So I guess I would say it is worth a try.

Mr. SCOTT. Well, we have dealt with this with telephones. You are familiar with, in Virginia, 18.2429, causing telephone to ring with intent to annoy——

Mr. O'NEIL. Yes.

Mr. SCOTT [continuing]. Where any person with or without the intent to communicate, but with intent to annoy, causes a telephone to ring is guilty of a misdemeanor crime.

Mr. O'NEIL. I think the intent to annoy may be troublesome for different reasons, and that is one of the reasons I suggested in 1966 that further attention to sharpening the intent elements would be a starting point, as well as targeting——

Mr. SCOTT. Well, we differentiate with telephone and mail. You can prohibit making somebody's telephone—you can prohibit ringing telephone communications that you probably couldn't prohibit mailing something because of the intrusion. Do we have the same problem with the Internet?

Mr. O'NEIL. We don't really know. When the Supreme Court, now 12 years ago, granted full first amendment protection to Internet speech, something they had not in decades done with respect to any other new medium, they left a lot of issues unanswered. And there are some downside implications, cyberbullying perhaps the most dramatic of which, we are only becoming aware, and on which the Supreme Court really has had no occasion to rule. So, again, I would say there have got to be some dark shadows in this generally promising penumbra called the Internet, and cyberbullying may be the darkest of them.

Mr. SCOTT. I have other questions, but I will defer at this time to the gentleman from Texas Mr. Gohmert.

Mr. GOHMERT. Thank you, Mr. Chairman.

And thank you for all of your testimony. Very thoughtful. And it does raise interesting issues.

Professor O'Neil, when you talk about intentional infliction of emotional distress, there are some States like Texas and in the legal literature of most places is an ongoing debate over whether or not that is sufficient to create a cause of action in tort law without some type of physical manifestation of the harm. So this would be taking that a couple of lightyears further down the road. We are going to jump past the physical manifestation of harm and go straight to making it a crime, which you say, as I understand you, it may fit here, but this is a troublesome horse to ride in for this.

Mr. O'NEIL. It certainly does raise questions. But your reference to the requirement of some discernible harm doesn't have to be suicide, doesn't have to be injury or heart attack. But it seems to me a conscientious prosecutor would never charge somebody under a cyberbullying statute without some fairly graphic evidence of impact or effect. I don't think that undermines the case; I just don't think it will be worth—would make sense to bring such a case unless there were evidence of effect or impact.

Mr. GOHMERT. Or unless somebody wanted to harass the harasser. And there have been prosecutors that went out of their way to seek indictments just to harass, as you, I am sure, know the old saying, a good prosecutor could indict a ham sandwich.

But without the public figure exception, then it does get interesting for us, because all Members of Congress are accused of all kinds of things. I get an e-mail my dad forwards regularly saying: If you guys would just get on Social Security, then it would solve the Social Security problem. They don't know we have been on Social Security for a number of years. And Ron Paul told me back in July that some liberal blog just put up that there was only one Member of Congress crazier than Ron Paul, and it was Louie Gohmert. So I don't know if that was meant to compliment or harass, but——

Mr. O'NEIL. Truth is a defense.

Mr. GOHMERT. Yeah, there is that.

And then you have got the situation where most everything that is on television or on video ends up on the Internet. And Sarah Palin would have all kinds of cause of actions, but do you really want to arrest David Letterman for a bad joke?

It creates troublesome issues here of what is not intended to harm, but intended to be humorous. And then practical jokes, those abound on the Internet. So it is a troublesome legal issue.

Now, I am intrigued, Ms. Willard, by your comments about maybe be more assistance through the block grants for the Safe Schools. Do you want to comment on that?

Ms. WILLARD. Yes. President Obama's budget—I am not sure everything that is going on there, but President Obama's budget zeroed out the funding for the States and local block grants for Safe Schools. They are redoing that program. My concern is that we have we have to move forward to address these issues of threats on line. The impact of these harmful actions is coming to school, and the programs that—the personnel, the expertise that is in place at the State and local level to address these issues are the Safe School folks.

Mr. GOHMERT. What about the adults that have similar problems?

Ms. WILLARD. Well, my focus is on teens. And maybe if we can get it during teens.

Mr. GOHMERT. They can teach their parents.

Ms. WILLARD. Yeah. But so within schools, we really need to have these Safe School programs, at least the State and local infrastructure funded, in order to be able to move forward to address these youth risk on-line issues. And then in the reauthorization of the Elementary and Secondary Education Act, we need to make sure that the Safe School plans are also addressing youth risk on line.

Mr. GOHMERT. Well, I see my time is about expired, but I really appreciate what you all bring to the debate, and it does pose some really interesting issues. But obviously there is a problem, as there always has been. And as one who was regularly beat up because I was small, but I wouldn't take stuff from the bigger guys, I am sensitive to bullying of any kind, and I don't want to overreact.

Ms. WILLARD. I went through junior high as Weirdo Willard, so we share that.

Mr. GOHMERT. Well, actually junior high is when I came out of my shell and started being a comedian back in those days. Not so funny anymore though.

But thank you, Mr. Chairman. I yield back.

Mr. SCOTT. Thank you.

The gentleman from California.

Mr. LUNGREN. Thank you, Mr. Chairman.

Mr. SCOTT. Thank you.

The gentlelady from Florida has just stepped back in. Thank you for deferring. The gentlelady from Florida.

Ms. WASSERMAN SCHULTZ. Thank you, Mr. Chairman. I had to take a call from our caucus Chairman. I apologize for stepping out a minute.

Ms. Westberg Warren, I, first of all, want to congratulate Web Wise Kids on all of the good work that your organization does, and I appreciate your assistance with the Internet safety education town halls that we have done in my congressional district. I can tell you that the way that your presenters interact with kids of all ages in age-appropriate ways, and the way the breakouts work separating parents and children is really a breakthrough for them, and it does lead to safer Internet behavior.

What I wanted to ask you is my good friend from Texas who needs truth as a defense made a reference to not thinking that we need a competitive grant program for Internet safety education, and this is just something that can be left up to parents and schoolteachers, and your colleague who is testifying with you today seems to imply that there is enough curricula out there, and that it isn't necessary to create anything else, and that everything is just fine.

So can you address those two comments, which I don't agree with, and I would imagine you don't either.

Ms. WARREN. Thank you for asking the question.

Yes, I absolutely do not agree with that. First of all, children really are our priority. They are our most valuable resource in this country, and we not only want to safeguard them on the Internet, but we want them to enjoy the Internet and thrive on it; and that, being able to thrive on it, is threatened if they are having serious consequences to their interaction on line.

The second thing is that there virtually is no funding out there. As an organization that has reached 7 million kids over the last several years, we are constantly looking for funding. Our programs cost a lot of money to produce because we are looking for effective ways to reach kids. One of the ways that we used to reach kids are using their own medium, computer games, and they are very costly to produce. So we are definitely as a nonprofit——

Ms. WASSERMAN SCHULTZ. But if you can address, why can't parents do it on their own? Why is it something that we need to be teaching in the schools? Why do we need to be creating Internet safety education programs to give tools to teachers and to parents to help them understand how they can reach their children?

Ms. WARREN. Because there is no current way that teachers are educated on how to implement Internet safety.

Ms. WASSERMAN SCHULTZ. So there is no comprehensive way?

Ms. WARREN. There is no comprehensive way.

Ms. WASSERMAN SCHULTZ. There is no continuing education programs. There is no consistent, comprehensive national approach to the curricula?

Ms. WARREN. No. But is a mandate. The E-Rate mandates that they have safety programs, and yet there is no funding for it. So parents are also critically important to this, but are oftentimes catching up to their children in their knowledge of technology. So empowering parents to be able to talk to their kids about Internet safety is critical, too.

Ms. WASSERMAN SCHULTZ. Thank you.

Ms. Willard, I have to tell you, I find it offensive that you would suggest that you would split hairs over whether Lori Drew was or was not home, was or was not involved in—I mean, she was convicted of a crime. It was later overturned, but she was—there was enough evidence for a jury and a judge to determine that she was culpable and significantly involved in events that led to the suicide of a young girl. And as mother of young girls, I find it offensive that you would suggest that that should just be cast aside and that it was unimportant.

It is also offensive to me for you to suggest that there is only 600 cyberbullying or—you made a reference to there being 600 instances of a particular type of bullying.

Ms. WILLARD. That was arrests for on-line sexual predation.

Ms. WASSERMAN SCHULTZ. All the worse then, because if it is your child that is the victim of that predation, it doesn't matter if it is 600, 6, or 1. If it is your child, it matters a whole lot. So I wouldn't—I really think it is offensive that you would trivialize the amount of—assuming that your numbers are even correct.

But let me get to your comments on my legislation. In your submitted testimony, you labeled it entirely unacceptable, and that is pretty strong language. Let me just be clear. I don't want to have an ineffective safety net program, and under my bill these are concepts that would be taught by Internet safety nonprofits, not police officers. You do understand that, right? You understand that this is information that would be imparted by Internet safety organizations. Okay. And one of the reasons that you are opposed to it is because you have—you oppose the funding from the Department of Justice.

Ms. WILLARD. No.

Ms. WASSERMAN SCHULTZ. Correct?

Ms. WILLARD. No. This needs to be funded and controlled jointly by the Department of Mental Health, by the Department of Education.

Ms. WASSERMAN SCHULTZ. But you don't want the grant program to be through the Department of Justice, correct?

Ms. WILLARD. It needs to be funded through all three.

Ms. WASSERMAN SCHULTZ. And, again, you think that these are concepts that would be taught by police officers? You do understand.

Ms. WILLARD. No. I understand that the intention of the bill—the concern I have is——

Ms. WASSERMAN SCHULTZ. No. I heard your concern in your testimony. But this is not a view that you have always held, correct?

Ms. WILLARD. I have always had concerns with the funding through the Department of Justice.

Ms. WASSERMAN SCHULTZ. Well, in fact, you supported.

Ms. WILLARD. And with the focus on——

Ms. WASSERMAN SCHULTZ. Well, in fact, you supported—on March 21, 2008, you sent out an action alert to your supporters when Senator Coburn put a hold on the very same bill that Senator Menendez is sponsoring this year, correct?

Ms. WILLARD. Yes.

Ms. WASSERMAN SCHULTZ. And in that e-mail, you begged for pressure from the field to be placed on Senator Coburn to release this hold. This is money that can come through the State and local education organizations as well as Internet safety organizations to support education. Those are your words, yes?

Ms. WILLARD. Uh-huh.

Ms. WASSERMAN SCHULTZ. And you are aware the bill you rallied for was funded through the Department of Justice, Yes?

Ms. WILLARD. Yes.

Ms. WASSERMAN SCHULTZ. Okay. Now, that was 2008. But, Ms. Willard, you supported the Menendez legislation when he and I unveiled it at a Senate press conference this May, didn't you?

Ms. WILLARD. Yes.

Ms. WASSERMAN SCHULTZ. Okay. You also forwarded Senator Menendez's office a press release that you sent to the Ed Tech Listserv, which again you stated you were exceptionally delighted with the language of the bill. Your words, right?

Ms. WILLARD. It was a significant improvement over the——

Ms. WASSERMAN SCHULTZ. But the words you used was "exceptionally delighted."

Ms. WILLARD. Yes.

Ms. WASSERMAN SCHULTZ. You don't seem exceptionally delighted today. And in that e-mail, you said we were headed in the right direction, and you recommended your followers contact their Representatives and Senators to support this legislation, correct?

Ms. WILLARD. Uh-huh.

Ms. WASSERMAN SCHULTZ. You also e-mailed reporters from the Associated Press and the New York Times asking them to write favorable stories about that legislation, our legislation, correct?

Ms. WILLARD. Correct.

Ms. WASSERMAN SCHULTZ. And that Senator Menendez and I were to be congratulated on this very positive step forward.

Ms. WILLARD. Yes.

Ms. WASSERMAN SCHULTZ. So at the very least, you would agree that you have been very inconsistent on this issue.

Ms. WILLARD. Correct.

Ms. WASSERMAN SCHULTZ. Okay. Well, it is hard for us to take your testimony seriously and treat you as an expert when you have been all over the board on the same bill with the same language.

Ms. WILLARD. This bill has been amended. The Menendez bill did not focus exclusively on Internet crime. This bill has now admitted an involvement with the Department of Education and the Department of Mental Health.

Ms. WASSERMAN SCHULTZ. The Menendez bill has not been amended. It is the same language.

Ms. WILLARD. Your bill is focusing solely on Internet crime.

Ms. WASSERMAN SCHULTZ. No, it is not. That is absolutely not the case.

Ms. WILLARD. We need to address——

Ms. WASSERMAN SCHULTZ. Have you read my bill?

Ms. WILLARD. Yes. We need to address——

Ms. WASSERMAN SCHULTZ. You have read the bill that is before this Committee?

Ms. WILLARD. Yes. We need to address these issues in a collaborative fashion, and it needs to involve the Department of Mental Health and the Department of Education.

Ms. WASSERMAN SCHULTZ. Well, this bill focuses on Internet safety education, not Internet crime. So I think you should reread the bill so that you can understand its focus better. And I would be more than happy to sit down with you and work with you to address some of your concerns. But I think we both have to be on the same page first before we haul off and criticize legislation that, A, we supported before and, B, we don't seem to understand today.

Thank you. I yield back the balance of my time.

Mr. SCOTT. Thank you.

And we had a couple of other questions. One, it seems to me that if we are going to reduce cyberbullying, it is a lot less complex dealing with the education program, as the gentlelady from Florida has offered, because you don't get into the constitutional quagmire.

Mr. Silverglate, are there constitutional problems in reducing cyberbullying with what are essentially education grants?

Mr. SILVERGLATE. No. I don't see any constitutional problems with that. I didn't even mention it in my testimony. That is just a question of whether you are likely to get your money's worth, and that is a judgment that I really don't have the experience to make.

Mr. SCOTT. Now, about every night you have cable news commentators insulting each other with the intent to harass or cause substantial emotional distress to each other. If they did that over the Internet, if that was streamed over the Internet, would that be a crime under H.R. 1966?

Mr. SILVERGLATE. Well, I do think that there are unforeseen dangers in this kind of legislation using terms which historically have given us a lot of difficulty in definition.

The thing about State common law jurisprudence is that it has been around a long time. Definitions have been honed over the centuries, and at various States we have a pretty good idea what we mean by "harassment." But the Federal—in Federal law, I think it is really an invitation to constitutional mischief. And since State law, it seems to me, does deal adequately with the problem of harassment, I don't know why we would be wanting to get into a whole new jurisprudential arena.

I think that the transfer, the movement of the harassment concept front the civil tort arena to the Federal criminal arena, it is just an invitation into what I call constitutional mischief, and a lot of people are going to end up convicted of crimes that I think most people in this room would agree should not be crimes. So it seems to me very problematic and no real benefit.

Mr. SCOTT. Now, is there a difference between e-mailing somebody directly and posting something somewhere on the Internet?

Mr. SILVERGLATE. One of the things that concerns me is that when Federal law, Federal legislation begins to focus on things like harassment or threats, it mostly focuses on the medium rather than on the actual act. So I think we are more afraid, if I can use that term "more afraid," of communications that go over channels that we are less familiar with, that society has less experience with. I think there is still a certain amount of cyber fear that goes into legislation such as is being proposed, and I think we should try to not focus so much on the medium and to focus instead on the substance of the communications.

You know, we had this idea that children are sitting in front of a screen, and Lord knows what they are saying, and Lord knows what they are reading and what they are doing. There is a certain amount of fear factor in that. If we try to factor that out, I think we will get back to the notion that State law really does handle this pretty well. It should not be a subject of Federal criminal interest.

Mr. SCOTT. When does posting things on the Internet become so harassing that it becomes a crime? Professor Palfrey, do you have a comment on constitutionality of posting things on the Internet that may—if somebody goes and looks at it, might be insulted and, because of youth, traumatized?

Mr. PALFREY. I certainly share the view that this is a horrible thing, and we should apply many approaches to address it. But I share Mr. Silverglate's view on the constitutionality question.

Mr. SCOTT. Mr. O'Neil, do you have any other comments on that?

Mr. O'NEIL. These cautions, I think, are very well taken. And the need for sharper definitions seems to me part of the next step in the maturation or development of 1966.

Mr. SCOTT. Would there a difference between posting something on the Internet?

Mr. O'NEIL. Yes. And that is why I specifically urge that one of the requirements of any such—one of the elements of any such offense should be evidence that a particular person or victim was targeted.

Mr. SCOTT. But you can have somebody's name posted.

Mr. O'NEIL. I don't think that is enough. It really has to be person-to-person evidence not only of the kind of intent that is spelled out in 1966, but a following paragraph which describes the process for identifying targeting of a particular person and then——

Mr. SCOTT. If you posted very insulting information on the Internet, and even if it is true, it can be traumatizing, invasion of privacy. How bad, how—where is the line between teasing and criminal?

Mr. O'NEIL. Nothing is said here about truth or falsehood, but I would assume that only harassing statements which were false and known to be false would satisfy the intent requirement of the first paragraph. And if it is simply teasing, or if it is true but being misused, if it is, let us say, an invasion of privacy, I don't think you ought to get beyond the first paragraph even to the consideration of targeting and impact or effect in the second——

Mr. SCOTT. Well, some things could be—you could be racially insensitive, appearance insensitive, and tease someone into the point of trauma.

Mr. O'NEIL. I don't think that is nearly enough. And such a statute, it seems to me, ought to be structured so that statements of that kind could not be caught. I think Mr. Silverglate issues a very strong warning, which I fully share, that a criminal law of this kind could be abused, it could be misused. It could pick up all sorts of just unpleasant adverse insults and so on. It has got to be written in such a way that that can't happen.

Mr. SCOTT. Ms. Warren, can truthful insults get to the point where they would be traumatizing?

Ms. WARREN. I believe so, yes, and especially if two teenagers. You know, you have to understand that as we are talking about teenagers, there are a lot of things still developing in their minds and in their hearts, and they are especially vulnerable during that time. Some of the things that happened, as we have heard today, can affect them for their entire lifetime.

Mr. SCOTT. Thank you.

Mr. Gohmert.

Mr. GOHMERT. Just briefly follow up on a couple of things. To follow up on that, one of the comments that has been—one of the things that has been discussed is the conveyance of naked pictures and then those being broadcast throughout the Internet. They are true pictures, they are accurate pictures, and yet the purpose was clearly to harass, intimidate, and belittle, hurt the individual who was in the pictures. So I get the impression that those—even though they are true and accurate, that that is not something that is going to be excluded under what is being proposed here, which, again, opens the door to a great deal of danger. So that is a concern.

I also wanted to make——

Mr. SCOTT. Would the gentleman yield?

Mr. GOHMERT. Yes. Sure.

Mr. SCOTT. I think the question would have to be asked in such a way that the picture was taken of an adult and transmitted to adults. Once you get into children, you have some opportunity to deal with it as child pornography. So long as it is not obscene for adults, you would have the constitutional problems.

Mr. GOHMERT. But the example being given is a juvenile having naked pictures of themselves transferred or sent to a boyfriend. So they are the ones that took them, they sent them. But then it was the release of those pictures publicly that was intended to harass and belittle, and that is a problem.

But I want to make sure everybody understood, under Federal laws, 18 U.S.C. 2261(a) prohibits an individual from using the mail, any interactive computer service, or any facility of interstate or foreign commerce to engage in a course of conduct that causes substantial emotional distress to that person or places that person in reasonable fear of death. 18 U.S.C. 875 makes it a crime punishable by up to 5 years in prison to transmit any communication in interstate or foreign commerce containing a threat to injure another person.

So there are some bills—some laws out there dealing with this issue to some extent. But I did want to make clear that my position was not mischaracterized. My friend Ms. Wasserman Schultz, I believe, has the very noblest of intentions with this proposal here. No question about her intent. It is nothing but noble and good. But I believe I understood her to characterize part of my position is, quote, that everything is just fine. And that is not my position. There is nothing fine about people being belittled, harassed, intimidated over the Internet or any other way.

So this is a rhetorical question that I would conclude with. But is this really an issue of lack of technical understanding of the Internet, or is it a lack of morality? Chuck Colson once said, you can't demand the morality of Woodstock and not expect a Columbine. If the morality is if it feels good, do it, then somebody is going to wonder if it feels good to belittle somebody over the Internet or shoot somebody or harm somebody. That will happen. We have got to come back around to a sense of morality that has been a problem throughout the ages.

But I thank you for the time and yield back.

Mr. SCOTT. Thank you.

Mr. Gohmert was reading the stalking prohibition, and it says: Causes substantial emotional distress or what we would call threats of serious bodily harm, which would be easy. But "causes substantial emotional distress." I think Professor O'Neil was saying that you would have to connect it with actual harm. And if you have actually caused substantial emotional distress, that would—that psychological damage would qualify for what you were talking about?

Mr. O'NEIL. It would have to be, I think, medically certified. It really would have to be provable, and it would have to be significant. Otherwise I just don't think it is a viable case.

Mr. SCOTT. Thank you.

I would like to thank our witnesses for their testimony today. Members may have additional written questions for the witnesses, which we will forward to you and ask that you answer as promptly as you can so that the answers may be part of the record.

We have received written testimony from the ACLU and from Baron Zoker and Adam Thayer, which will be included in the record, without objection.

Without objection, the hearing record will remain open for 1 week for the submission of additional materials.

And, without objection, the Subcommittee stands adjourned.

[Whereupon, at 5:05 p.m., the Subcommittee was adjourned.]

APPENDIX

MATERIAL SUBMITTED FOR THE HEARING RECORD

Statement of Chairman John Conyers, Jr.
Hearing on Cyberbullying
Before the Subcommittee on Crime, Terrorism, and Homeland Security
Wednesday, September 30, 2009 at 3 p.m.
2141 Rayburn House Office Building

Cyberbullying, an important issue that deserves discussion by government at all levels.

I commend our colleagues, Representatives Sánchez and Wasserman Shultz, for each introducing bills on this subject, and I thank them for testifying here today, as well as Representative Culberson, who is the cosponsor of the bill introduced by Representative Wasserman Schultz.

These Members have made an important contribution to bringing attention to the problem of cyberbullying.

I want to discuss the bills briefly, and speak to issues which we need to keep in mind as we decide whether legislation is necessary to deal with the problem of cyberbullying.

First, Congresswoman Sánchez has introduced H.R. 1966, the Megan Meier Cyberbullying Prevention Act. This bill would create a new federal crime for sending electronic communications "with the intent to coerce, intimidate, harass, or cause substantial emotional distress" to someone "in order to support severe, repeated, and hostile behavior."

Penalties for this crime range from fines to imprisonment for up to two years.

With respect to this bill, I caution that we need to be careful any time the government gets involved with the regulation of speech. The First Amendment applies to all of us, including kids. I understand our witnesses today will discuss the free speech issues in connection with cyberbullying.

We want to protect our children from harm, but we also don't want to harm their rights, even if it is their right to say something unkind, as kids sometimes do.

Second, Congresswoman Wasserman Shultz and Congressman Culberson have introduced H.R. 3630, the AWARE Act. This bill would create a grant program to be implemented by the Justice Department. Grants would be awarded to organizations to carry out "internet crime awareness and cybercrime prevention" programs.

They would be aimed at preventing not only cyberbullying, but also other types of dangerous behavior that children sometimes engage in on the

Internet.

Of course I encourage efforts to prevent children from engaging in dangerous or hurtful behavior. I particularly support programs which involve multi-disciplinary approaches that include parents and educators in the process.

Third, as we consider legislative approaches to this issue, we need to keep in mind that most conduct that experts define as cyberbullying occurs between minors. Whenever this Committee considers legislation that applies to juveniles, we must be extremely careful.

As medical science generates more sophisticated research on brain development, we learn more about the differences between the brains of juveniles and adults.

Our laws need to recognize these differences and the unique ways juveniles interact socially as we think about creating new criminal provisions that would apply to juvenile behavior.

I thank the witnesses for being here today and I look forward to the testimony on this important issue.

WASHINGTON
LEGISLATIVE OFFICE

September 30, 2009

Chairman Robert C. Scott	Ranking Member Louie Gohmert
Subcommittee on Crime Terrorism,	Subcommittee on Crime Terrorism,
and Homeland Security Membership	and Homeland Security Membership
U.S. House of Representatives	U.S. House of Representatives
Washington, DC 20515	Washington, DC 20515

Re: Subcommittee hearing on 'Cyberbullying and Other Online Safety Issues for Children'
H. R. 1966, the "Megan Meier Cyberbullying Prevention Act"
H. R. 3630, the "Adolescent Web Awareness Requires Education Act (AWARE Act)"

AMERICAN CIVIL
LIBERTIES UNION
WASHINGTON
LEGISLATIVE OFFICE
915 15th STREET, NW, 6TH FL
WASHINGTON, DC 20005
T/202.544.1681
F/202.546.0738
WWW.ACLU.ORG

Dear Chairman Scott and Ranking Member Gohmert:

On behalf of the American Civil Liberties Union (ACLU), we offer this statement for the record in connection with the Crime Subcommittee's hearing on 'Cyberbullying and Other Online Safety Issues for Children', H. R. 1966, the "Megan Meier Cyberbullying Prevention Act", and H. R. 3630, the "Adolescent Web Awareness Requires Education Act (AWARE Act)." The ACLU is a non-partisan organization with more than a half million members, countless additional activists and supporters, and 53 affiliates nationwide. While recognizing the concern many Americans have about reported incidents of online bullying of young people, we urge the Subcommittee to avoid taking steps that would criminalize protected first amendment speech and, instead, to support programs that would educate and inform children, parents and educators about online risk prevention and Internet safety practices.

The Internet presents new ways for people to communicate with each other – but it does not inherently change behaviors associated with intimidation and harassment that have been present in human society for centuries. Reported incidents of online harassment have produced heartbreaking stories with which all Americans sympathize. From these reports, one can conclude that online harassment is on the rise. But it is also well-documented that online communication generally is increasing exponentially and so it is only logical that incidents of online bullying would also be increasing.

Interpersonal harassment has not come into existence by virtue of the Internet – it is safe to assume that it has been around as long as humans have inhabited the earth. People have harassed and intimidated others face to face, through third parties, through the mails, by telephone, across the airwaves, and – now – via Internet communications. This does not serve to minimize the problems associated with Internet-based bullying and harassment of young people. Rather, it demonstrates that the focus should be on the bullying and harassing behavior and not on the means by which it is communicated. To think that serious harassment only occurs online is to miss the true nature of the phenomenon. The parent of one victim of harassment recognized as much when he said, "Even though what happened to [my son] happened online as well, it really started in school. I think that's the first step that a lot of states are missing."[1]

Criminalizing speech online is unconstitutional and will be ineffective. Harassing speech will either continue online in violation of the law or it will simply shift to other spheres within which it simultaneously exists. Moreover, the scope of 'bullying' speech is likely to fall short of the constitutional standard requiring the existence of a 'true threat'.[2] H. R. 1966, for example, criminalizes online speech intended to intimidate a person, among other things. Unfortunate as it may be, many communications are intended to be intimidating to one degree or another – but should not be rendered criminal in nature. Can a lawyer vigorously assert a client's rights in email communications to opposing counsel? Can a radio listener send an email to a call-in show vigorously disagreeing with something said on air? Certainly they should be able to do so – especially in the absence of making a personal threat to do harm.

Courts have looked to whether the speech in question is a true threat.[3] Many of these cases reflect truly disturbing communications – but not all of them are deemed to be the kind of actual threat sufficient to justify restricting an individual's right to speak freely. In the case of most bullying behaviors – including most cyber-bullying, it is not at all clear that the communications can be viewed as the kind of threat that courts say justifies federal proscription. An attempt to ban such behavior must be narrowly drawn and it must closely define its terms so that there is no question – in the minds of law enforcement or in the minds of the general population – precisely what types of communication are banned.

A better approach, in our view, is to inform children, parents, and educators about the risks and opportunities associated with online communications. H. R. 3630 and related bill H. R. 3222 both have elements aimed at doing so. The latter bill, in particular, would direct grant funds to the development of Internet safety education programs and would provide training and tools to teachers and parents to help keep young people in a position to use the Internet safely. The former bill – H. R. 3630 – puts a greater emphasis on crime awareness which in our view misplaces priorities about the Internet, which should be viewed as a vast and expanding resource and not primarily as a place of criminality and intimidation. However, the bill also includes some of the same opportunities for education of children, parents and educators and, as such, represents a better step forward than an overbroad attempt to criminalize certain kinds of online speech.

---

[1] Surdin, Ashley, In Several States, A Push to Stem Cyber-Bullying, Washington Post (Jan. 1, 2009)

[2] Watts v. U.S., 394 U.S. 705, 707 (1969). While the Watts case dealt with a threat ultimately deemed to be political speech, it serves as the foundation point for the notion that a limitation on free speech rights demands that the harassing speech be a 'true threat'.

[3] *Id.; see also, e.g.,* Planned Parenthood v. American Coalition of Life Activists, 290 F.3d 1058 (9th Cir. 2002); U. S. v. Alkhabaz, 104 F.3d 1492 (6th Cir. 1997).

We do not take issue with the Subcommittee's interest in looking at the issues of harassment and intimidation, but we would encourage taking a broad view of the phenomenon, not limited to the particular tools of communications used to convey such threats. For example a review of the tools that the Internet can provide to assist in limiting bullying, such as documentation of incidents and identifying when intervention is necessary, could yield valuable additional tools for fighting the problem. If additional legislation at the federal level is deemed necessary, we would urge the Subcommittee to carefully define its terms before moving forward, taking care to draw any prohibitions very narrowly so as to avoid limitations on protected First Amendment rights. In the meantime, as we still stand on the opening threshold of the Internet age, there is much good that can be done by expanding public awareness of both the benefits and risks associated with online activity and we would encourage the Subcommittee to support such efforts.

If you have questions or comments on ACLU's position on this issue, please feel free to contact me at mmacleod@dcaclu.org.

Sincerely,

Michael W. Macleod-Ball
Acting Director, Washington Legislative Office

cc: Subcommittee members

Written Testimony of

Berin Szoka & Adam Thierer

Senior Fellows & Directors,

Center for Internet Freedom &

Center for Digital Media Freedom,

The Progress & Freedom Foundation

Before the

U.S. House Committee on the Judiciary

Subcommittee on Crime, Terrorism & Homeland Security

Hearing on

Cyber Bullying and other Online Safety Issues for Children;

H.R. 1966, the "Megan Meier Cyber Bullying Prevention Act"; and

H.R. 3630, the "Adolescent Web Awareness Requires Education Act (AWARE Act)"

September 30, 2009

THE PROGRESS & FREEDOM FOUNDATION

Written Testimony of Berin Szoka & Adam D. Thierer,* Senior Fellows & Directors, Center for Internet Freedom & Center for Digital Media Freedom, The Progress & Freedom Foundation

Before the U.S. House Committee on the Judiciary
Subcommittee on Crime, Terrorism & Homeland Security;
Hearing on Cyber Bullying and other Online Safety Issues for Children;
H.R. 1966, the "Megan Meier Cyber Bullying Prevention Act"; and
H.R. 3630, the "Adolescent Web Awareness Requires Education Act (AWARE Act)"
September 30, 2009

As Senior Fellows at The Progress & Freedom Foundation Paper (PFF), we published a (PFF) white paper entitled "Cyberbullying Legislation: Why Education is Preferable to Regulation" last June. We are grateful to Chairman Scott and Ranking Member Gohmert for the opportunity to submit written comments as part of the record for today's hearing on "Cyber Bullying and other Online Safety Issues for Children." Our paper, included in adapted and updated form, discusses both of the bills before the committee today.

We take seriously the rising online safety concerns about child online safety, which are more well-founded than previous fears about online predation, which have been greatly overblown. Evidence suggests that cyberbullying is on the rise and can have profoundly damaging consequences for children.

In the wake of a handful of high-profile cyberbullying incidents that resulted in teen suicides, some state lawmakers began floating legislation to address the issue. Before the Committee today are two very different federal approaches. One approach, found in Rep. Sánchez's the "Megan Meier Cyber Bullying Prevention Act" (H.R. 1966), is focused on the creation of a new federal felony to punish cyberbullying, which would include fines and jail time for violators. The other approach, found in Rep. Wasserman Schultz's "Adolescent Web Awareness Requires Education Act (AWARE Act)" (H.R. 3630) is education-based and would create a education grant program to address issues of cybercrime affecting children, including cyber bullying, in schools and communities. We note the following in comparing these two approaches:

- Criminalizing what is mostly child-on-child behavior will not likely solve the age-old problem of kids mistreating each other, a problem that has traditionally been dealt with through counseling and rehabilitation at the local level.
- Any attempt at criminalization would raise thorny speech and due process issues related to legal definitions of harassing or intimidating speech. In certain cases where an adult egregiously harasses someone they know is a child over the Internet, criminal sanctions might be appropriate, yet narrowly tailoring such a law would be extremely difficult.

* The views expressed here are their own, and are not necessarily the views of the PFF board, other fellows or staff.

1444 EYE STREET, NW ▪ SUITE 500 ▪ WASHINGTON, D.C. 20005
202-289-8928 ▪ mail@pff.org ▪ www.pff.org

- Even if such a law could be written to minimize First and Fourteenth Amendment concerns, a critical question of federalism would remain: Should the federal government assert control of an issue of criminal law that has traditionally been left to the states? This is not merely a constitutional question, but a practical one: The federal criminal justice system simply is not equipped to accommodate juvenile defendants. For this reason and because it is still unclear how to write a narrowly tailored law, if criminal sanctions are pursued as a solution, it may be preferable to defer to state experimentation with varying models at this time.
- By contrast, education and awareness-based approaches have a chance of effectively reducing truly harmful behavior, especially over the long haul. Such approaches would have the added benefit of avoiding constitutional pitfalls and subsequent court challenges. Thus, if the Committee truly desires to address cyberbullying and online cybercrime concerns related to children at this time, it is clear that criminalization/regulation is, at best, premature and that education is the better approach.
- Some legal academics and practitioners have proposed to restrict the immunity from tort law created by Section 230 of the Communications Decency Act as a way of addressing concerns about online child safety, including cyberbullying. Yet the basic premise behind Section 230 remains just as true today as it was in 1996: Holding online intermediaries liable for the speech or conduct of users of their sites or services would strongly discourage voluntary efforts to police online communities. Indeed, as social networking functionality has become ubiquitous online, Section 230 has grown *more* important as a "Cornerstone of Internet Freedom": Without it, online intermediaries would be forced to take sweeping steps that could massively chill online speech and threaten the viability of smaller site operators.

For the Committee's consideration, we have submitted the complete text of our recent paper, "Cyberbullying Legislation: Why Education is Preferable to Regulation." This report is also available at the Progress & Freedom Foundation's website, www.pff.org.

We would be happy to respond to any questions that members of the Committee or their staff might have. We can be reached at bszoka@pff.org and athierer@pff.org.

THE PROGRESS & FREEDOM FOUNDATION

Cyberbullying Legislation: Why Education is Preferable to Regulation

Berin Szoka & Adam Thierer

Table of Contents

I. Introduction: Focusing on the Real Threats to Online Child Safety

Concerns about online child safety continue to motivate calls for legislative action at both the federal and state level.[1] In the 110th session of Congress, for example, more than 30 measures

1. Adam Thierer, The Progress & Freedom Foundation, *Congress, Content Regulation, and Child Protection: The Expanding Legislative Agenda*, Progress Snapshot 4.4, Feb. 6, 2008, www.pff.org/issues-pubs/ps/2008/ps4.4childprotection.html.

were introduced aimed at addressing child safety concerns in one way or another, although only a few of them passed into law.[2]

Social networking safety has been a particular concern in recent years. Fears of predators lurking online created a veritable "techno-panic" and spawned various legislative responses.[3] At the federal level, lawmakers introduced legislation to ban access to social networking sites in schools and libraries.[4] At the state level, several state attorneys general pushed for age verification mandates to exclude those over or under a certain age from accessing social networking sites.[5] More recently, some state lawmakers have advocated expanded "parental consent" requirements that would essentially expand upon the model established by the federal Children's Online Privacy Protection Act (COPPA) of 1998.[6] Although none of these measures have yet been implemented, such proposals continue to be floated.

Importantly, recent research by academics and online child safety task forces has found that these concerns are being somewhat over-stated. In particular, the "techno-panic" over online predators and abduction has been largely unwarranted.[7] The most authoritative data available from the Crimes against Children Research Center (CCRC) at the University of New Hampshire (UNH) finds that, although arrests of online predators increased between 2000 and 2006, "most arrests and the majority of the increase involved offenders who solicited undercover

---

2. John Morris & Adam Thierer, Center for Democracy & Technology and The Progress & Freedom Foundation, *Online Child Protection & Online Content Regulation Bills in the 110th Congress*, June 13, 2008, www.pff.org/issues-pubs/books/110thSafetyContentBillsCDT-PFF.pdf.

3. Alice Marwick, *To Catch a Predator? The MySpace Moral Panic*, First Monday, Vol. 13, No. 6-2, June 2008, www.uic.ecu/htbin/cgiwrap/bin/ojs/index.php/fm/article/view/2152/1966; Wade Roush, *The Moral Panic over Social Networking Sites*, Technology Review, Aug. 7, 2006, www.technologyreview.com/communications/17266; Adam Thierer, Progress & Freedom Foundation, *Technopanics and the Great Social Networking Scare*, PFF Blog, June 10, 2008, http://blog.pff.org/archives/2008/07/technopanics_an.html; Anne Collier, *Why Techopanics are Bad*, Net Family News, April 23, 2009, www.netfamilynews.org/2009/04/why-technopanics-are-bad.html.

4. In the 109th Congress, former Rep. Michael Fitzpatrick (R-PA) introduced the Deleting Online Predators Act (DOPA), which proposed a ban on social networking sites in public schools and libraries. DOPA passed the House of Representatives shortly thereafter by a lopsided 410-15 vote, but failed to pass the Senate. The measure was reintroduced just a few weeks into the 110th Congress by Senator Ted Stevens (R-AK), the ranking minority member and former chairman of the Senate Commerce Committee. It was section 2 of a bill that Sen. Stevens sponsored, entitled the "Protecting Children in the 21st Century Act" (S. 49), but was later removed from the bill. *See* Declan McCullagh, *Chat Rooms Could Face Expulsion*, CNet News.com, July 28, 2006, http://news.com.com/2100-1028_3-6099414.html?part=rss&tag=6099414&subj=news.

5. *See, e.g.*, Emily Steel & Julia Angwin, *MySpace Receives More Pressure to Limit Children's Access to Site*, Wall Street Journal, June 23, 2006, http://online.wsj.com/public/article/SB115102268445288250-YRxktOrTsyyf1QIQf2EPBYSf7IU_20070624.html; Susan Haigh, *Conn. Bill Would Force MySpace Age Check*, Yahoo News.com, March 7, 2007, www.msnbc.msn.com/id/17502005.

6. 15 U.S.C. §§ 6501–6506. *See* Berin Szoka & Adam Thierer, The Progress & Freedom Foundation, *COPPA 2.0: The New Battle over Privacy, Age Verification, Online Safety & Free Speech*, Progress on Point 16.11, May 2009, *available at* http://pff.org/issues-pubs/pops/2009/pop16.11-COPPA-and-age-verification.pdf.

7. *See supra* note 3. Lenore Skenazy, author of *Free-Range Kids: Giving Our Children the Freedom We Had Without Going Nuts with Worry*, notes that, "the chances of any one American child being kidnapped and killed by a stranger are almost infinitesimally small: .00007 percent." Lenore Skenazy, *Free-Range Kids: Giving Our Children the Freedom We Had Without Going Nuts with Worry* at 16 (2009).

investigators, not actual youth."[8] "Online predator arrests comprise only 1 percent of arrests for sex crimes committed against minors," says Janis Wolak, a CCRC senior researcher and co-director of the National Juvenile Online Victimization Studies. "The recent growth in arrests is best explained by increasing numbers of youth online,[9] migration of crime from offline to online venues and the intensification of law enforcement activity against online crimes," Wolak says.[10] The UNH researchers thus conclude:

> The publicity about online "predators" who prey on naive children using trickery and violence is largely inaccurate. Internet sex crimes involving adults and juveniles more often fit a model of statutory rape—adult offenders who meet, develop relationships with, and openly seduce underage teenagers—than a model of forcible sexual assault or pedophilic child molesting. This is a serious problem, but one that requires different approaches from current prevention messages emphasizing parental control and the dangers of divulging personal information. Developmentally appropriate prevention strategies that target youth directly and focus on healthy sexual development and avoiding victimization are needed. These should provide younger adolescents with awareness and avoidance skills, while educating older youth about the pitfalls of relationships with adults and their criminal nature. Particular attention should be paid to higher risk youth, including those with histories of sexual abuse, sexual orientation concerns, and patterns of off- and online risk taking.[11]

II. Cyberbullying: A Genuine Problem

The picture that is emerging from academic research suggests that peer-on-peer cyberbullying is a more significant online safety concern than child predation—and that this problem is growing. A recent report produced by the Internet Safety Technical Task Force, a blue ribbon task force assembled in 2008 by state AGs to study online safety, concluded that "Bullying and harassment, most often by peers, are the most frequent threats that minors face, both online and offline."[12]

---

8. Crimes against Children Research Center, University of New Hampshire, *Trends in Arrests of Online "Predators,"* March 2009, www.unh.edu/ccrc/pdf/CV194.pdf.

9. The percentage of Americans under age 18 using the Internet was growing significantly during this period, from 73 percent to 93 percent. *See* Larry Magid, *Study Has Mostly Good News about Predator Risk*, CNet News.com, March 31, 2009, http://news.cnet.com/8301-19518_3-10208135-238.html.

10. Janis Wolak, David Finkelhor & Kimberly Mitchell, Crimes against Children Research Center, University of New Hampshire, *National Study Finds Large Increase in Arrests of Online Predators in Undercover Operations*, March 31, 2009, www.unh.edu/ccrc/Presspacket/033109_pr.pdf.

11. Janice Wolak, David Finkelhor, Kimberly Mitchell & Michele Ybarra, *Online "Predators" and their Victims: Myths, Realities and Implications for Prevention and Treatment*, 63 Am. Psychologist 2, 111-128 (2008), www.unh.edu/ccrc/pdf/Am%20Psy%202-08.pdf.

12. Internet Safety Technical Task Force, Enhancing Child Safety & Online Technologies: Final Report of the Internet Safety Technical Task Force to the Multi-State Working Group on Social Networking of State Attorneys

Because of these findings as well as some high-profile press stories about particularly extreme cases of online harassment resulting in child suicides over the past year, cyberbullying has become the child safety issue *du jour*. Although a precise definition is elusive,[13] cyberbullying expert Nancy Willard, Executive Director of the Center for Safe and Responsible Internet Use, offers the following general definition:

> Cyberbullying is being cruel to others by sending or posting harmful material or engaging in other forms of social cruelty using the Internet or other digital technologies. It has various forms, including direct harassment and indirect activities that are intended to damage the reputation or interfere with the relationships of the student targeted, such as posting harmful material, impersonating the person, disseminating personal information or images, or activities that result in exclusion.[14]

Parry Aftab, founder of Wired Safety and StopCyberBullying.org, defines cyberbullying specifically as cyberharassment or cyberstalking committed by kids against kids—not by adults against kids or against other adults[15]—a critical distinction discussed below in Section VI.A.[16]

Research has also suggested that more emotionally damaging incidents of cyberbullying are closely related to offline aggression. Both perpetrators and targets in cyberbullying incidents demonstrated significant psychosocial concerns, including increased involvement with alcohol and drugs, friends involved in delinquent behavior, anger responses, and involvement in offline relational, physical, and sexual aggression. There is also a significant interplay between bullying and retaliation—online and at school.[17]

General of the United States, Dec. 31, 2008, at 4, http://cyber.law.harvard.edu/sites/cyber.law.harvard.edu /files/ISTTF_Final_Report-Executive_Summary.pdf. Full disclosure: Adam Thierer was a member of this task force.

13. Dr. Robin Kowalski, a professor of psychology at Clemson University, notes that, "In part because of the relatively recent research on cyber bullying, investigators have yet to reach a consensus on how to define cyber bullying and what time parameters to impose when assessing prevalence (within a couple of months vs. lifetime prevalence). Thus, it is not surprising that reports of cyber bullying show considerable variability." Robin Kowalski, *Cyber Bullying: Recognizing and Treating Victim and Aggressor*, Psychiatric Times, Vol. 25 No. 11, Oct. 1, 2008, www.psychiatrictimes.com/display/article/10168/1336550.

14. Nancy Willard, *Cyberbullying Legislation and School Policies: Where are the Boundaries of the "Schoolhouse Gate" in the New Virtual World?*, March 2007, www.cyberbully.org/cyberbully/docs/cblegislation.pdf

15. *What is cyberbullying, exactly?*, www.stopcyberbullying.org/what_is_cyberbullying_exactly.html (last accessed on June 10, 2009).

16. "Cyberbullying generally refers to harassment occurring *among school-aged children* through the use of the Internet." Alison M. Smith, Congressional Research Service, *Protection of Children Online: Federal and State Laws Addressing Cyberstalking, Cyberharassment, and Cyberbullying*, Sept. 5, 2008, at 10, http://assets.opencrs.com/rpts/RL34651_20080905.pdf [*hereinafter* CRS Report].

17. *See generally* Center for Disease Control and Prevention, *Youth Violence and Electronic Media: Similar Behaviors, Different Venues*?, Journal of Adolescent Health, Dec. 2007 Supplement, www.jahonline.org/content/suppl07; Sameer Hinduja & Justin W. Patchin, *Bullying Beyond the Schoolyard: Preventing and Responding to Cyberbullying*, (2009), www.corwinpress.com/booksProdDesc.nav?prodId=Book232981; Jaana Juvonen & Elisheva F. Gross, *Extending the*

Worse yet, there is ample evidence that bullying is a risk factor that can lead young people to commit suicide. In a recent review of studies of bullying and suicide, researchers at the Yale School of Medicine found signs of an apparent connection between bullying, being bullied and suicide in children. Almost all of the studies found connections between being bullied and suicide.[18] Indeed, two recent suicides by 11-year olds who were the victim of anti-gay bullying at school illustrated that this problem is not unique to the online environment.[19] But not just the victims were in danger: Kids who bully other kids are also at increased risk for suicide.

Thus, concerns about cyberbullying are certainly more well-founded than previous fears about predators lurking online. Not all legislative responses to the problem are equal, however. Two bills recently introduced in Congress offer very different approaches to the problem: education and regulation. Comparing these bills and considering their effects make it clear that regulation is, at best, premature and that education is the better approach.

III. Approach #1: A New Federal Cyberbullying Crime

In October 2006, a Missouri girl named Megan Meier hanged herself less than a month before her fourteenth birthday. She had been exchanging MySpace messages for over a month with "Josh Evans," the persona of a 16-year old boy who claimed to live nearby. In the version of the incident reported in widespread news coverage, Josh Evans was the creation of Lori Drew, the mother of one of Meier's classmates and a neighbor of the Meier family. Drew reportedly used the Josh Evans persona to build a relationship with Meier, an emotionally fragile and socially isolated girl, before turning nasty, and telling Meier, just before her suicide, "You are a bad person and everybody hates you. Have a shitty rest of your life. The world would be a better place without you."[20]

County officials considered prosecuting Drew under Missouri's harassment law, but ultimately declined to do so.[21] Their decision not to prosecute Drew bears closer examination in light of the version of this incident reported widely by most media outlets, which ultimately drove the introduction of the federal bill that now bears Megan Meier's name. Jack Banas, the St. Charles

---

School Grounds? Bullying Experiences in Cyberspace. Journal of School Health, Vol. 78, Issue 9, 2008, www3.interscience.wiley.com/journal/121371836/abstract?.

18. *Bullying And Being Bullied Linked To Suicide In Children, Review Of Studies Suggests*, ScienceDaily, July 19, 2008, www.sciencedaily.com/releases/2008/07/080717170428.htm.

19. *See* Susan Donaldson James, *When Words Can Kill: 'That's So Gay': Anti-Gay Taunts in School Lead to 11-Year-Old's Suicide and Rising Calls for Change*, April 14, 2009, http://abcnews.go.com/Health/MindMoodNews/story?id=7328091&page=1.

20. Steve Pokin, *'My Space' Hoax Ends with Suicide of Dardenne Prairie Teen*, Suburban Journals, Nov. 1, 2007, http://suburbanjournals.stltoday.com/articles/2007/11/11/news/sj2tn20071110-1111stc_pokin_1.ii1.txt.

21. Steve Pokin, *No Charges to be Filed over Meier Suicide*, Suburban Journals, Dec. 3, 2007, http://suburbanjournals.stltoday.com/articles/2007/12/03/news/doc47543edb763a7031547461.txt. *See also CRS Report*, *supra* note 16 at 11 (noting that Missouri's harassment statute did not apply to cyberharassment at the time of Drew's conduct, but that this statute has since been updated to include electronic communications). *See infra* at note 60 and associated text (noting that the current Missouri statute would make cyberbullying among kids a misdemeanor).

County (Missouri) prosecuting attorney indicated that while there were conflicting statements on whose idea it was to create the fake account, Lori Drew consistently maintained that it was not her idea. Ashley Grills, an 18-year-old friend of the Drew family, indicated that creating the account was Ms. Drew's idea, but also was found to have changed her story in other aspects. At trial, Grills admitted that she created the fake "Josh Evans" account and that most of the conversations between Meier, including the last one before her suicide, were with Grills, not Lori Drew.[22] According to *Wired*, "the revelation [was] ... at odds with the government's position that the 49-year-old Drew took a leading role in creating a MySpace account," and Grills's "testimony seemed to undermine the government's case."[23] Incidentally, Banas indicated that his findings were in accord with an investigation by the Federal Bureau of Investigation, which also looked into the matter.[24]

Notwithstanding the conclusions of these law enforcement agencies, the U.S. Attorney's office in Los Angeles charged Drew with unauthorized access to MySpace's computers, using the federal anti-hacking Computer Fraud & Abuse Act. Prosecutors argued that violating MySpace's terms of service for the purpose of harming another was the legal equivalent of computer hacking.[25] Drew was cleared of the felony computer-hacking charges, but convicted of three misdemeanors for unauthorized computer access. At the time of this writing, the U.S. District Court judge was still weighing a defense motion to overturn the jury verdict in the case.[26]

This case received widespread media attention, especially as Meier's grieving parents called for legislation to punish such harassment in the future. In May 2008, Rep. Linda Sánchez introduced the "Megan Meier Cyberbullying Prevention Act," which would create a new federal felony:

> Whoever transmits in interstate or foreign commerce any communication, with the intent to coerce, intimidate, harass, or cause substantial emotional distress to a person, using electronic means to support severe, repeated, and hostile behavior, shall be fined under this title or imprisoned not more than two years, or both. [...]
>
> the term "communication" means the electronic transmission, between or among points specified by the user, of information of the user's choosing, without change in the form or content of the information as sent and received; ...

22. Kim Zetter, *Government's Star Witness Stumbles: MySpace Hoax Was Her Idea, Not Drew's*, Wired Threat Level, Nov. 20, 2008, www.wired.com/threatlevel/2008/11/lori-drew-pla-3.

23. *Id.*

24. *Supra* note 21.

25. *See CRS Report, supra* note 16 at 11.

26. Kim Zetter, *Judge Postpones Lori Drew Sentencing, Weighs Dismissal*, Wired Threat Level, May 18, 2009, www.wired.com/threatlevel/2009/05/drew_sentenced/26.

> the term "electronic means" means any equipment dependent on electrical power to access an information service, including email, instant messaging, blogs, websites, telephones, and text messages.[27]

The Sánchez bill identifies the harm at issue as follows:

> (3) Electronic communications provide anonymity to the perpetrator and the potential for widespread public distribution, potentially making them severely dangerous and cruel to youth.
> (4) Online victimizations are associated with emotional distress and other psychological problems, including depression.
> (5) Cyberbullying can cause psychological harm, including depression; negatively impact academic performance, safety, and the well-being of children in school; force children to change schools; and in some cases lead to extreme violent behavior, including murder and suicide.
> (6) Sixty percent of mental health professionals who responded to the Survey of Internet Mental Health Issues report having treated at least one patient with a problematic Internet experience in the previous five years; 54 percent of these clients were 18 years of age or younger.

In defending her bill, Rep. Sánchez argues that, while existing laws criminalize "stalking, sexual harassment, identity theft and more when it takes place in person and online," cyberbullying is "one serious online offense that has no penalty." She insists that "When so-called free speech leads to bullies having free-reign to threaten kids, it is time to act."[28]

While no one would doubt Rep. Sánchez's desire to respond to concerns of emotional harm being inflicted upon children and teens, her legislation sets up a starkly different standard for online bullying as compared to offline bullying. If the statements made in the Lori Drew case were made on a playground, the perpetrator might face a stern conversation with the principal and possibly suspension. Since kids who bully other kids are themselves at increased risk for suicide, such perpetrators might also receive the special counseling attention they need. But if the same comment were sent via email or posted on a social networking site, such a bully would be subject to potential federal prosecution under Rep. Sánchez's bill. Consequently, that individual would face the prospect of a felony sentence of two years' incarceration in a federal prison, even though this has traditionally not been the approach applied to real-world bullying—and is significantly harsher than the approach taken in Missouri in response to the

27. Megan Meier Cyberbullying Prevention Act, H.R. 1966, 111th Congress, (April 2, 2009), http://thomas.loc.gov/cgi-bin/query/z?c111:H.R.1966::. The bill was originally introduced as H.R. 6123 on May 22, 2008, *available at* http://frwebgate.access.gpo.gov/cgi-bin/getdoc.cgi?dbname=110_cong_bills&docid=f:h6123ih.txt.pdf.

28. Linda Sánchez, *Protecting Victims, Preserving Freedoms*, Huffington Post, May 6, 2009, www.huffingtonpost.com/rep-linda-Sánchez/protecting-victims-preser_b_198079.html.

Megan Meier tragedy.[29] The task of counseling and rehabilitation has traditionally been administered at the state and local level—and not on the federal level.

Given the degree to which the most emotionally distressing cyberbullying incidents involve a combination of both online and offline hurtful interactions, how would a federal prosecutor determine when the online communications had reached the stage where the child cyberbully should face such prosecution?

Thus, while there is a clear need to address the full range of bullying behavior, the criminalization of just one manifestation of such bullying behavior (that is, the online variety) seems misguided.

IV. Approach #2: Education, Awareness-Building, Prevention & Intervention

There is an alternative to the regulatory approach outlined in the Sánchez bill: Lawmakers could get serious about supporting online safety education, awareness-building efforts, prevention, and intervention. Such an approach has recently been floated in both chambers of Congress. In mid-May, the "School and Family Education about the Internet (SAFE Internet) Act" (S. 1047) was introduced in the Senate by Sen. Robert Menendez (D-NJ).[30] Rep. Debbie Wasserman Schultz (D-FL) has introduced a companion bill in the House entitled the "AWARE Act."[31] The House measure proposes an Internet crime education grant program that will be administered by the Department of Justice. These agencies will also work in consultation with education groups, Internet crime awareness and cybercrime prevention groups, and other relevant experts in the field of new media and child safety to administer a five-year grant program, under which each grant will be awarded for a two-year period. Eligible non-profits may use the grants to:

(1) identify, develop, and implement Internet crime awareness and cybercrime prevention programs, including educational technology, multimedia and interactive applications, online resources, and lesson plans;

(2) provide professional training to elementary and secondary school teachers, administrators, and other staff on crime awareness and cybercrime prevention;

(3) educate parents about teaching their children how to protect themselves from becoming victims of Internet crime;

(4) develop Internet crime awareness and cybercrime prevention programs for children;

---

29. *See infra* note 60 and associated text (noting that the current Missouri statute would make cyberbullying among kids a misdemeanor, not a felony).

30. Office of Sen. Robert Menendez, *Keeping Children and Teens Safe Online: Sen. Menendez, Rep. Wasserman Shultz Propose National Grand Program for Internet and Wireless Safety Education*, May 13, 2009, http://menendez.senate.gov/newsroom/record.cfm?id=312958&. The text of the act is *available at* http://thomas.loc.gov/cgi-bin/query/z?c111:S.1047:.

31. Available at http://thomas.loc.gov/cgi-bin/query/D?c111:1:./temp/~c111UMdW3O::

(5) train and support peer-driven Internet crime awareness and cybercrime prevention initiatives;

(6) coordinate and fund research initiatives that investigate online risks to children and Internet crime awareness and cybercrime prevention; or

(7) develop and implement public education campaigns to promote awareness of crimes against children on the Internet and the prevention of such crimes.[32]

V. Choosing a Path Forward: Questions Congress Should Consider

Legislators face essentially four questions in responding to cyberbullying:

1. Do we need new laws to deal with the problem?
2. Should those laws be implemented at the federal or state level?
3. What should the laws look like?
4. What are the downsides of varying approaches?

Rep. Sánchez obviously believes that a federal criminal law is needed. But even if she is correct that current laws are inadequate to punish cyberbullying, and that a federal law is appropriate, it by no means follows that a new federal *criminal* law is the answer, or that her bills strikes the right balance between legitimate child protection concerns and free speech. Examination of her bill and existing state and federal laws makes clear how thorny these issues are.

At the very least, serious thought needs to be given to crafting a better bill before Congress continues down the path of federal regulation. In the short term, a better solution might emerge if left up to experimentation by the states, even if a federal bill is eventually needed because of the uniquely interstate nature of the Internet and the possibility of conflicting state standards.

Thus, at present, if federal lawmakers feel compelled to do something to address this concern, education and awareness-building efforts represent the superior option.

VI. Problems with the Sánchez Bill

A. Defining the Problem: Cyberbullying, Cyberharassment & Cyberstalking

Rep. Sánchez's rhetoric—both in the bill's proposed Congressional Findings and in her public statements about the bill—emphasizes the harm to children. But the bill itself makes no distinction as to the age of the victim. As John Morris, Director of the Internet Standards, Technology and Policy Project at the Center for Democracy & Technology, has noted:

> the bill is aimed at protecting children, but in fact the crime created has no such focus or limitation, and squarely applies to harsh adult-to-adult communications (such as can happen in, for example, broken romantic relationships). Such adult

32. SAFE Internet Act, *supra* note 30 § 4(d).

communications should not be a federal crime, and the [bill] should not clothe a sweeping new crime in the rhetoric of protecting minors.[33]

Again, while the definition of cyberbullying is still evolving, the best definition focuses on peer-on-peer harassment or stalking *of kids by kids*.[34] Indeed, this was precisely the definitional conclusion reached by a Congressional Research Service report that Rep. Sánchez herself apparently commissioned.[35] In this sense, the Sánchez bill is not really about "cyberbullying" at all, but about the broader problems of cyberharassment and cyberstalking. While the definitions of all three terms are still evolving,[36] treating cyberbullying as the minor-on-minor subset of harassment/stalking is critical because it reflects very real differences between abusive communications by adults and by kids, which in turn suggest that remedies appropriate for adult perpetrators may not be appropriate for kid perpetrators—such as the criminal sanctions Sánchez proposes.

Furthermore, an important distinction should be drawn between harassment and stalking. Like harassment, stalking generally requires a pattern or course of conduct (in criminal law, the "*mens reus*" or bad act).[37] But stalking generally also requires a specific "*mens rea*" (bad intention): "the goal of a stalker is to exert 'control' over the victim by instilling fear in [them]."[38] Thus, as noted by the CRS Report that Rep. Sánchez commissioned, stalking laws generally require either that the perpetrator make a "credible threat" or that the course of conduct would cause a "reasonable person" to fear for their safety.[39] The *mens rea* defined by

---

33. John Morris, Center for Democracy & Technology, *Memorandum to Interested Parties Re: H.R. 1966, the Megan Meier Cyberbullying Prevention Act*, June 9, 2009.

34. *See supra* note 14.

35. "Cyberbullying generally refers to harassment occurring *among school-aged children* through the use of the Internet." *CRS Report*, *supra* note 16 at 10 (emphasis added). CRS Reports must be commissioned by a Member of Congress, but do not mention which member commissioned a particular report. However, at a panel discussion held on June 12, 2009 by the Family Online Safety Institute entitled "FOSI Panel Series: Is it Possible to Legislate Safety?," Mercedes Salem, the Sánchez staffer who apparently drafted H.R. 1966, noted that her office had commissioned this report.

36. *See, e.g.*, Darby Dickerson, *What is Cyberbullying*, NASPA Leadership Exchange, Vol. 29, Spring 2009, *available at* http://papers.ssrn.com/sol3/papers.cfm?abstract_id=1375150.

37. Some states follow essentially the same distinctions, but apply different terminology. For example, in Missouri, mere stalking is repeated harassment, while a credible threat means the difference between stalking and "aggravated stalking." *See* Mo. Rev. Stat. §§ 565.225, 565.090. Thus, the only substantive difference is that Missouri might treat a single communication as "harassment," rather than requiring a series of communications.

38. Naomi Harlin Goodno, *Cyberstalking, a New Crime: Evaluating the Effectiveness of Current State and Federal Laws*, 72 Mo. L. Rev. 125, 127 (2007), www.law.missouri.edu/lawreview/docs/72-1/Goodno.pdf.

39. *Id.* at 133-34. CRS Report, *supra* note 16 at 9 ("Generally, cyberharassment differs from cyberstalking in that a credible threat is not involved"). *See also* U.S. Department of Justice, Office of Justice Programs, Violence Against Women Office, Report to Congress, May 2001, www.ncjrs.gov/pdffiles1/ojp/186157.pdf.

> Stalking generally involves harassing and threatening behavior that an individual engages in repeatedly, such as following a person, appearing at a person's home or place of business, making harassing phone calls, leaving written messages or objects, or vandalizing a person's property. Most stalking laws require the perpetrator to make a credible threat of violence

the Sánchez bill is the "intent to coerce, intimidate, harass, or cause substantial emotional distress to a person."[40] Thus, besides addressing conduct aimed *at* adults, the bill attempts to criminalize both cyberharassment and cyberstalking *by* adults.

Good arguments can be made for laws against either cyberbullying or cyberstalking generally (in the sense used above) because the former involves kids, who are particularly vulnerable, and the latter involves threats or fears of physical violence. Such laws, if carefully drafted, might even be consistent with the First Amendment. But instead of seeking such a narrowly tailored approach, Rep. Sánchez has written a sweeping cyber*harassment* statute in the guise of a cyberbullying statute. While she purports to have consulted with First Amendment experts, it is difficult to see how her approach (making all cyberharassment a federal felony) can be reconciled with the First Amendment. Let us first consider her approach as written and then consider her approach if limited to cyberharassment *of kids*.

B. Constitutional Concerns about the Sánchez Bill

While Rep. Sánchez insists that her bill is constitutional, the CRS Report she commissioned identifies a number of problems posed by the bill under the First and Fourteenth Amendments, as have other legal scholars.

First, the CRS Report concludes that criminalizing harassment, as distinct from stalking (where a "true threat" is made), would "likely.... be deemed constitutionally deficient."[41] As UCLA Law School professor Eugene Volokh has noted, Sánchez's bill does not fall into recognized exemptions to First Amendment protection of speech because it is not limited to threats of violence, applying equally to stalking and harassment. Under the bill's broad scope, "much constitutionally protected speech" would be affected by the Sánchez bill if it is "said with an intent to coerce or substantially distress, is severe, is hostile, and is repeated."[42]

Rep. Sánchez's staff has defended the bill by drawing an analogy to the 1994 federal Violence Against Women Act (VAWA) (18 U.S.C. § 2261A), which prohibits using "the mail, any interactive computer service, or any facility of interstate or foreign commerce to engage in a course of conduct that causes substantial emotional distress to that person or places that person in reasonable fear of ... death." Until being amended in 2006, VAWA applied only to stalking (requiring that the victim feel a reasonable fear of physical harm) and did not apply to online activities.[43] In 2000, the Supreme Court upheld the criminal sanctions portion of the original VAWA,[44] but the constitutionality of the 2006 amendments has not yet been

---

against the victim. Others include threats against the victim's immediate family, and still others require only that the alleged stalker's course of conduct constitute an implied threat.

40. *See supra* note 27.

41. *CRS Report, supra* note 16 at 13-15.

42. Eugene Volokh, *Rep. Linda Sánchez Defends Proposed Outlawing of Using Blogs, the Web, Etc. To Cause Substantial Emotional Distress Through "Severe, Repeated, and Hostile" Speech*, Huffington Post, May 7, 2009, www.huffingtonpost.com/eugene-volokh/rep-linda-Sánchez-defends_b_199556.html.

43. *See* Violence Against Women and Department of Justice Reauthorization Act of 2005, P.L. 109-162 Tit. I, § 113, 119 Stat. 2960 (2006); *see also CRS Report*, supra note 16 at 8.

44. United States v. Morrison, 529 U.S. 598 (2000) (striking down VAWA's civil remedies).

determined by any federal court.[45] But even if VAWA's application to "substantial emotional distress" and online communications were ultimately upheld, the 2006 VAWA amendments differ significantly from the approach of the Sánchez bill. In particular, VAWA requires both intent to make the victim suffer, and that the victim *actually* suffer, either fear of physical injury or substantial emotional distress. By contrast, the Sánchez bill applies to all communications made with "the intent to coerce, intimidate, harass, *or* cause substantial emotional distress." Thus, the Sánchez bill would sweep in a vast range of communications that neither cause, nor are intended to cause, "substantial emotional distress," but that are merely made with intent to "coerce," "intimidate" or "harass."

Neither of the other two federal statutes discussed by the CRS Report provides a clear analogy in support of the Sánchez approach. The first statute (18 U.S.C. § 875) has been applied to some Internet communications, but requires both a threat of physical harm and extortion—and therefore would not apply to mere harassment, or even most stalking.[46] The second statute (47 U.S.C. § 223) applies to e-mail and to harassment without any threat, but only to anonymous, direct communication between perpetrator and victim. While Sánchez claims that her bill is focused on anonymous communications,[47] in fact her bill makes no such distinction. The courts have upheld this statute's application to "communications intended to instill fear in the victim, not to provoke a discussion about political issues of the day," but according to the CRS Report, "have yet to address this statute as it applies to Internet 'harassment.'"[48]

Even if there were a constitutional way to criminalize "harassment" (absent a "true threat"), attempting to distinguish between actual harassment and what may be nothing more than routine online "flaming" (*i.e.*, heated online exchanges) is no easy task. In particular, the Sánchez bill offers no clear standard by which judges and juries should distinguish between unprotected "coercion" (say, e-mail harassment of an ex-boyfriend) and "coercion" in an effort to get someone to change a political or philosophical position (say, repeated and hostile blog postings).[49] The physical separation made possible by the Internet makes it difficult to easily apply traditional legal norms, including even well-settled definitions. This makes it especially important to craft clear definitions that can survive a constitutional analysis for vagueness. Indeed, the CRS Report concludes by recommending that key terms be defined in any legislation to avoid vagueness or subjectivity that would create "an inordinate amount of prosecutorial discretion"—something that Rep. Sánchez, despite her professed commitment to constitutional values, has not bothered to add to her bill in the nine months that have elapsed since the release of the CRS Report.[50]

Second, as Volokh notes, the bill offers no clear standard by which to distinguish between injuries to public and private figures—a key distinction in First Amendment jurisprudence.

---

45. *See CRS Report, supra* note 16 at 7.
46. *See id.* at 6-7.
47. Sánchez, *supra* note 28.
48. *CRS Report, supra* note 16 at 8-9 (quoting United States v. Bowker, 372 F.3d 365 (6th Cir. 2004)).
49. Volokh, *supra note* 42.
50. *CRS Report, supra* note 16 at 24.

While Rep. Sánchez responds that juries would have "discretion" to make such distinctions, Volokh points out that "unguided jury discretion is itself a First Amendment problem, because of the risk that juries will apply the law in viewpoint-based ways." He also observes that, whatever one might say about "coercive" speech towards public figures, "even speech that distresses private people is generally constitutionally protected."

Third, as Volokh notes, the bill sets a dangerous precedent for further erosions of free speech rights, particularly because, unlike many state laws, the bill does not specifically exclude constitutionally protected speech.[51]

Finally, the CRS Report notes that these concerns about statutory vagueness may also cause cyberharassment/stalking/bullying laws to run afoul of the Fourteenth Amendment's due process guarantees:

> Criminal statutes that lack sufficient definiteness or specificity may be held "void for vagueness." Under this doctrine, a governmental regulation or statute may be declared void if it fails to give a person adequate warning that his or her conduct is prohibited or if it fails to set out adequate standards to prevent arbitrary and/or discriminatory enforcement.[52]

Given these concerns, any proposal to criminalize certain forms of speech will require that extraordinary care be taken to avoid creating vagueness and subjectivity.

C. No Easy Remedy for Additional Problems with the Sánchez Bill

What if the Sánchez bill were truly focused on cyberbullying by limiting its scope to kids? Limiting the bill's scope to intentionally and exceptionally harmful communications directed at kids under a certain age would clearly help to remedy some of the most severe First Amendment problems raised by the current bill by minimizing the chilling of constitutionally protected speech. Indeed, if one read only the name of her bill, the "Megan Meier Cyberbullying Prevention Act," one might assume (wrongly) that the bill was focused on harassment by older adults of kids young enough to be truly vulnerable—but also old enough to respond to bullying through something as extreme as suicide.

Whatever Lori Drew's precise involvement, the Megan Meier case seems to be an exception to the rule that most cyberbullying incidents involve peer-on-peer interaction among youth. But the prospect of even a few adults tormenting children to the point of suicide would rouse the righteous indignation of anyone. Narrowly crafting a law to deal with this specific problem would well be worthwhile if it prevents another Megan Meier from taking her own life.

But how to write such a law is by no means clear. What should the standard for harassment be? What age range of victims should we protect? What age range of perpetrators should we punish? These are difficult questions that may require more empirical data to answer, and it

51. *Cf.* Mo. Rev. Stat. § 565.225 ("Constitutionally protected activity is not included within the meaning of 'course of conduct.' Such constitutionally protected activity includes picketing or other organized protests.").

52. *CRS Report, supra* note 16 at 20-21.

might be better to allow the states to explore them and experiment with legislation before Congress blindly leaps forward with a poorly-crafted law that could seriously chill constitutionally protected online expression. We discuss existing Missouri and other state laws herein only because they illustrate how some states have dealt with some of these questions, not because they should serve as a comprehensive model. Indeed, state laws vary widely, as noted by the CRS Report,[53] and a careful study of that survey should be undertaken before even attempting to propose any one-size-fits-all legislative solution. But four prerequisites are clear.

First, criminal sanctions should be limited to adult perpetrators. The criminalization approach found in the Sánchez bill might sound like a way to "get serious" about protecting kids, but its effect would fall most directly on kids themselves. Creating a criminal record—especially a *federal felony*, as Rep. Sánchez proposes—for peer-on-peer harassment could stigmatize kids for life for mistakes made during their youth. The problem of peer-on-peer harassment (true "cyberbullying" in the sense used herein) should be addressed through "less restrictive" means like education and awareness-building—such as would be supported by as the SAFE Internet Act. Furthermore, to the extent that cyberbullying occurs between students at the same school, appropriate disciplinary and counseling policies at the school level involving pediatric professionals may significantly improve the problem.[54] Indeed, ensuring that schools have the legal authority to develop and implement such policies (consistent with the First and Fourteenth Amendments) is the most compelling need for legislation at the moment.[55]

Second, the class of victims protected by criminal (and especially felony) sanctions should be limited to minors. The most obvious analogy is offered by the federal telephone harassment law cited above (47 U.S.C. § 223), which applies not only to anonymous, harassing communications, but also to the transmission of "any… communication which is obscene or child pornography… [made] knowing that the recipient of the communication is under 18 years of age."[56] Another analogy is offered by COPPA, which applies to the collection of information from kids under 13.[57] While this cut-off may be too low, and certainly would not have applied to Megan Meier, the age of majority (18) may be too high. Perhaps 16 and under might be more appropriate. This was the cut-off chosen by Congress when it passed the ill-fated Children's Online Protection Act (COPA), which has been struck down by various courts on First Amendment grounds.[58] It was also the age range initially contemplated for COPPA, which would originally have required parental notification—but not prior consent—for the collection of information about children ages 13-16. Some states use such cut-offs to distinguish between

53. *Id.* at 25-34 (cataloguing state cyber harassment and cyberstalking laws)

54. "Parents of these [bullied] children need to be encouraged to demand that schools take action, and pediatricians probably need to be ready to talk to the principal. And we need to follow up with the children to make sure the situation gets better, and to check in on their emotional health and get them help if they need it." Perri Klass, M.D., *At Last, Facing Down Bullies and Their Enablers*, N.Y. Times, June 8, 2009, www.nytimes.com/2009/06/09/health/09klas.html?_r=2&emc=eta1.

55. *See CRS Report, supra note* 16 at 10-11 (discussing such statutes recently enacted).

56. 47 U.S.C. § 223(a)(1)(B). *See supra* at 13.

57. *See supra* note 6.

58. *See infra* note 70.

degrees of stalking (and therefore penalties). For example, Alaska considers it stalking in the first degree if, among other things, the victim is 15 or under—another potential cut-off.[59]

While choosing an appropriate cut-off would be difficult, equally difficult would be determining how to avoid chilling communication among near-age peers. For example, if the law applies to victims 16 and under, but also to perpetrators 17 and older, it might significantly affect a great deal of legitimate interaction among kids. The better approach would be to leave a gap large enough between the maximum age of victims (say, 16 and under) and the minimum age of perpetrators (say, 21 and over) to ensure that the law really does focus on genuine harassment by mature adults and not interaction between younger kids and older kids or very young adults. While current Missouri law unwisely criminalizes *all* cyberharassment, including cyberbullying, it does provide a useful example as to how to draw distinctions by age, creating precisely such a gap: The law deems it a felony (with a sentence of up to four years) if the perpetrator is 21 or over and the victim is 17 or under, and otherwise treats interactions without credible threats as misdemeanors (with a sentence of up to one year).[60] For interactions among kids, or between young adults in this gap and kids, there may be better solutions than criminalization such as better user policies for online social networks or codes of conduct for schools.

Third, the law should require, as 47 U.S.C. § 223 does, that the adult knew, or had reason to know, that their victim was below a certain age at the time of the cyberharassment. Given the inherent anonymity of the Internet, this requirement would be essential to ensure that a well-intentioned law does not chill protected speech (since users often do not know with whom they are really communicating or how old that person is). Again, Missouri provides just one example of how to write such a law, defining one variety of harassment as "Knowing[] communicat[ion] with another person who is, or who purports to be, seventeen years of age or younger...."[61]

Fourth, for the reasons discussed above, the law should provide unambiguous standards to ensure that it does not burden protected speech or violate the Fourteenth Amendment's due process guarantees. Determining precisely how to do that will require careful engagement with First and Fourteenth Amendment experts.

In all these cases, rather than rushing to respond to media headlines, Congress should think very carefully if it is to write laws that will both survive constitutional challenges and actually work in the real world without disrupting legitimate online speech and conversations. Again, to return to the four major questions outlined above, even if we conclude that a new law is indeed needed and that it should be federal, it is by no means clear what the law should actually look like. That is sufficient reason for Congress to, as the CRS Report commissioned by Rep. Sánchez suggests, "adopt a wait-and-see approach, monitoring state Internet harassment-related activities and the types of behavior prosecuted," instead of rushing to pass pre-emptive federal legislation.[62]

---

59. www.legis.state.ak.us/cgi-bin/folioisa.dll/stattx99/query=*/doc/{t3744}/pageitems={body}?.
60. *See* Mo. Rev. Stat. § 565.090(2)(1) (harassment),; 565.225(3)(4) (stalking), and 558.011 (sentences).
61. Mo. Rev. Stat. § 565.090(1)(4).
62. *CRS Report, supra* note 16 at 23.

VII. Advantages of the Wasserman Schultz Bill

As illustrated above, the Sánchez bill raises more questions than it answers. Rather than rushing to regulate without clear answers to these difficult questions, Congress can make a clear contribution to concerns about cyberbullying today by taking an "educate first" approach to the issue.

The only real shortcoming of the Wasserman Schultz bill is that, while it embraces education and awareness-building as superior options to treating kids like criminals, it nonetheless vests primary grant-making authority in the Department of Justice (DOJ) rather than, say, the Departments of Education or Health and Human Services. Because government agencies tend to award grants to agencies they are most familiar with and because grant proposals inevitably tend to reflect the likely interests of grant-makers, vesting this authority in the Department of Justice is likely to mean that the educational efforts funded under the bill will be more focused on the model of treating cyberbullies as perpetrators.

Nonetheless, even if the DOJ is driving the grant-making process, such an education-based approach is still the more sensible approach compared to what is found in the Sánchez bill. Incidentally, there are other federal education-based efforts currently underway. The "Protecting Children in the 21st Century Act," which was signed into law by President Bush in 2008 as part of the "Broadband Data Services Improvement Act,"[63] required that the Federal Trade Commission (FTC) "carry out a nationwide program to increase public awareness and provide education" to promote safer Internet use and:

> utilize existing resources and efforts of the Federal Government, State and local governments, nonprofit organizations, private technology and financial companies, Internet service providers, World Wide Web-based resources, and other appropriate entities, that includes (1) identifying, promoting, and encouraging best practices for Internet safety; (2) establishing and carrying out a national outreach and education campaign regarding Internet safety utilizing various media and Internet-based resources; (3) facilitating access to, and the exchange of, information regarding Internet safety to promote up to-date knowledge regarding current issues; and, (4) facilitating access to Internet safety education and public awareness efforts the Commission considers appropriate by States, units of local government, schools, police departments, nonprofit organizations, and other appropriate entities.[64]

Moreover, this same bill authorized the creation of an Online Safety and Technology Working Group (OSTWG).[65] Pursuant to the requirements of the bill, the National Telecommunications and Information Administration (NTIA) at the Commerce Department has appointed 35

---

63. Broadband Data Services Improvement Act of 2008, Pub. L. 110-385, 110th Congress.

64. For background on how these measures originated in Congress, *see* Adam Thierer, The Progress & Freedom Foundation, *Two Sensible, Education-Based Approaches to Online Child Safety*, Progress Snapshot 3.10, Sept. 2007, www.pff.org/issues-pubs/ps/2007/ps3.10safetyeducationbills.pdf.

65. Full disclosure: Adam Thierer is a member of the OSTWG task force.

members who will serve 15-month terms to study the status of industry efforts to promote online safety, best practices among industry leaders, the market for parental control technologies, and assistance to law enforcement in cases of online child abuse. The Department of Justice, the U.S. Department of Education, the Federal Communications Commission, and the Federal Trade Commission all have delegates serving on the working group. OSTWG began its work in early June 2009 and is due to report back to Congress within one year.[66]

A. Advantages of an Education-Based Approach

The reason educational-based approaches are so vital is because they can help teach kids how to behave in—or respond to—a wide variety of situations. Education teaches lessons and builds resiliency, providing skills and strength that can last a lifetime.

That was the central finding of a blue-ribbon panel of experts convened in 2002 by the National Research Council of the National Academy of Sciences to study how best to protect children in the new, interactive, "always-on" multimedia world. Under the leadership of former U.S. Attorney General Richard Thornburgh, the group produced a massive report that outlined a sweeping array of methods and technological controls for dealing with potentially objectionable media content or online dangers. Ultimately, however, the experts used a compelling metaphor to explain why education was the most important strategy on which parents and policymakers should rely:

> Technology—in the form of fences around pools, pool alarms, and locks—can help protect children from drowning in swimming pools. However, teaching a child to swim—and when to avoid pools—is a far safer approach than relying on locks, fences, and alarms to prevent him or her from drowning. Does this mean that parents should not buy fences, alarms, or locks? Of course not—because they do provide some benefit. But parents cannot rely exclusively on those devices to keep their children safe from drowning, and most parents recognize that a child who knows how to swim is less likely to be harmed than one who does not. Furthermore, teaching a child to swim and to exercise good judgment about bodies of water to avoid has applicability and relevance far beyond swimming pools—as any parent who takes a child to the beach can testify.[67]

Regrettably, we often fail to teach our children how to swim in the "new media" waters. Indeed, to extend the metaphor, it is as if we are generally adopting an approach that is more akin to just throwing kids in the deep end and waiting to see what happens. Educational initiatives are essential to rectifying this situation.

---

66. *See* Leslie Cantu, *Newest Online Safety Group Will Report on Industry Efforts*, Washington Internet Daily, Vol. 10 No. 107, June 5, 2009; Larry Magid, *Federal Panel Takes a Fresh Look at Kids' Internet Safety*, San Jose Mercury News, www.mercurynews.com/business/ci_12522370?nclick_check=1; Adam Thierer, The Progress & Freedom Foundation, *Online Safety Technology Working Group (OSTWG) Is Underway*, PFF Blog, June 4, 2009, http://blog.pff.org/archives/2009/06/online_safety_technology_working_group_ostwg_is_un.html.

67. Computer Science and Telecommunications Board, National Research Council, *Youth, Pornography, and the Internet* (National Academy Press, 2002) at 224, www.nap.edu/openbook.php?isbn=0309082749&page=224.

B. Education-Based Approaches Are Clearly Constitutional

Such education-based legislative approaches have the added benefit of remaining within the boundaries of the First and Fourteenth Amendments because government would not be seeking to restrict speech, but simply to better inform and empower parents regarding the parental control tools and techniques already at their disposal.[68] The courts have encouraged—or demanded—such educational efforts, and not just in the case of online safety.[69]

This is why education, not regulation, represents the superior approach to address online child safety. When Congress seeks to regulate online speech or content, by contrast, such measures usually get bogged down in the courts for many years. For example, the Child Online Protection Act (COPA) was passed by Congress in 1998 in an effort to restrict minors' access to adult-oriented websites. After a decade-long series of court battles about the constitutionality of the measure, in January 2009, the U.S. Supreme Court rejected the government's latest request to revive COPA, meaning it is likely dead.[70] (It had already been considered by the Supreme Court twice before). If all the money that has been spent litigating this case had instead been spent on media literacy and online safety campaigns, it could have produced concrete, lasting results.

VIII. Child Safety & Proper "Netiquette": The Role of Parents & Schools

A. The Role of Parents

While government-directed or funded educational efforts can play an important role in addressing online safety concerns, there is simply no substitute for parental oversight and mentoring.

One of the most important parenting responsibilities involves teaching our children basic manners and rules of social etiquette. For example, we teach them proper dinner table manners, to cover their mouths when they cough or sneeze, to hold doors open for others, or simply to say "thank you" when given something. When we become parents, no government

---

68. "Although government's ability to regulate content may be weak, its ability to promote positive programming and media research is not. Government at all levels should fund the creation and evaluation of positive media initiatives such as public service campaigns to reduce risky behaviors and studies about educational programs that explore innovative uses of media." Jeanne Brooks-Gunn & Elisabeth Hirschhorn Donahue, *Introducing the Issue*, Children and Electronic Media, The Future of Children, Vol. 18, No. 1, Spring 2008, at 8.

69. For example, in a November 2006 decision which struck down an Illinois law that sought to regulate video game sales to minors, the Seventh Circuit Court of Appeals noted that parents are already actively involved in making decisions about the games their children buy. Noting how parents are involved in well over 83 percent of their children's video game purchases, the court went on to argue that:

> If Illinois passed legislation which increased awareness of the ESRB [Entertainment Software Rating Board voluntary rating] system, perhaps through a wide media campaign, the already-high rate of parental involvement could only rise. Nothing in the record convinces us that this proposal would not be at least as effective as the proposed speech restrictions.

Entertainment Software Association v. Blagojevich, 7th Cir. Court of Appeals, WL 3392078, November 27, 2006, p. 16, www.jenner.com/files/tbl_s18News/RelatedDocuments147/2652/Seventh_Circuit_ILVideoGame.pdf.

70. *See* Adam Thierer, Progress & Freedom Foundation, *Closing the Book on COPA*, *PFF Blog*, Jan. 21, 2009, http://blog.pff.org/archives/2009/01/closing_the_boo.html.

agent gives us a handbook instructing us to do all this. Rather, these are social conventions that come to us naturally, just as they did with our parents and the generations of parents that came before them. These informal social rules of etiquette are essential to well-functioning civil society. And it is commonly understood that these are "rules" that families, communities, and other social groups or institutions are primarily responsible for instilling in children.

Why should it be any different for proper technology usage? It shouldn't. Again, most parents repeatedly drill basic manners into their kids until it is clear that they "get it." Unfortunately, the same cannot always be said for online manners. This might be the case because the Internet and digital communications technologies have taken the world by storm and caught the current generation of parents a bit off guard. Unaccustomed to, or uncomfortable with modern computing or communications devices, some parents may be neglecting their duties in terms of teaching good online etiquette and basic online safety.[71] Of course, as the panel of experts assembled by the National Academy of Sciences also noted, "It may be that as today's children become parents themselves, their familiarity with rapid rates of technological change will reduce the knowledge gap between them and their children, and mitigate to some extent the consequences of the gap that remains."[72]

Nonetheless, here are a few lessons children need to be taught as they begin using interactive communications and computing technologies, including mobile phones,[73] mobile media devices, interactive video games, instant messaging, social networking websites, blogs, and so on. To begin, kids need to be taught to assume that *everything* they do in the digital, online world could be archived *forever* and will be available to their future employers, romantic interests, children and grandchildren, and so forth.[74] This admonition needs to be repeated frequently to remind minors that their online actions today could have profound consequences tomorrow. Beyond this warning, children need to be encouraged to follow some other sensible rules while using the Internet and other interactive technologies:

- ✓ Treat others you meet online with the same respect that you would accord them in person;
- ✓ Do not bully or harass your peers;

---

71. "People naturally fear what they do not understand," says Jason Illian, author of *MySpace, MyKids*. But, "regardless of how you feel about the Internet and online communities, they are here to stay... Likewise, we're not going to stop our teenagers from chatting online and meeting new people. We just need to teach them how to do it properly so that they don't get hurt." Jason Illian, *MySpace, MyKids* (2007) at 10-11.

72. *CRS Report, supra* note 67 at 49.

73. The National Institute on Media and the Family produces an excellent guide for parents entitled *Cell Phones and Your Kids* that offers friendly pointers for parents looking to teach their children proper cell phone etiquette. *See* National Institute on Media and the Family, *A MediaWise Parent Guide—Cell Phones and Your* Kids, 2006, www.mediafamily.org/network_pdf/cellphon_guide.pdf. Also, the Harvard University Center on Media and Child Health has some useful guidelines at http://cmch.tv/mentors/hotTopic.asp?id=70.

74. "The biggest message that must be imparted to children and teens with respect to [their] privacy and the Internet is: *It's not private!!!* Anything and everything that is put into electronic form and sent or posted online is public or could easily be made public. Think before you post." Nancy E. Willard, *Cyber-Safe* Kids, *Cyber-Savvy Teens* (2007), at 92 (emphasis original).

- ✓ Avoid using lewd or obscene language online or in communications;
- ✓ Do not post negative comments about your teachers or principals online;
- ✓ Do not post or share inappropriate pictures of yourself or others;
- ✓ Be extremely careful about talking to strangers online;
- ✓ Do not share your personal information with unknown parties; and
- ✓ Talk to parents and educators about serious online concerns and report dangerous situations or harassing communications to them.

Parents might want to formalize such guidelines in the home and then devise penalties if their children break those rules (perhaps by taking away PCs, mobile phones, or other digital devices for a period of time).

Finally, there are many other sites and organizations that offer useful tips for dealing with cyberbullying, including: Cyberbulling.us,[75] the Center for Safe and Responsible Internet Use,[76] Cyberbullyhelp.com,[77] ConnectSafely.org,[78] the National Crime Prevention Council,[79] Wired Safety,[80] StopBullyingNow.com,[81] and the Anti-Defamation League.[82]

B. The Role of Schools

Schools also have an important role to play. Because the most emotionally damaging bullying incidents generally involve young people who are interacting with each other at school, it is imperative that schools take proactive leadership in addressing the concerns of bullying behavior. Even though there are some First Amendment constraints on how far they can go, schools clearly have the authority to respond to bullying behavior that occurs on campus. There are greater restrictions when the harmful speech occurs off-campus. However, courts facing the question of school district authority to respond to off-campus speech have consistently held that schools may, if given the appropriate statutory authority mentioned above, regulate the speech of their students outside school through formal discipline "if it would substantially disrupt school operations or interfere with the right of others."[83]

---

75. www.cyberbullying.us
76. www.cyberbully.org/cyberbully
77. www.cyberbullyhelp.com
78. www.connectsafely.org/safety-tips/safety-tips/index.php?option=com_content&task=view&id=1390&Itemid=95
79. www.ncpc.org/cyberbullying
80. www.stopcyberbullying.com
81. www.stopbullyingnow.com
82. www.adl.org/education/curriculum_connections/cyberbullying
83. As summarized by the Third Circuit:

    a school may categorically prohibit lewd, vulgar or profane language on school property. Under *Hazelwood* [*School District v. Kuhlmeier*, 484 U.S. 260 (1988)], a school may regulate schools-sponsored speech (that is, speech that a reasonable observer would view as the school's own speech) on the basis of any legitimate pedagogical concern. "Speech falling outside of these

Further, these legal standards only address the imposition of a formal disciplinary sanction. There are no constitutional restrictions whatsoever on schools' ability to implement comprehensive bullying prevention programs that would address both on-campus and online bullying behavior. Many schools have implemented bullying prevention programs in association with their violence prevention activities through the Safe and Drug Free Schools programs.[84]

Indeed, states are also moving to incorporate a requirement in their state statutes that requires schools to incorporate cyberbullying prevention into overall bullying prevention policies and prevention activities. The Anti-Defamation League has recently provided model legislation to accomplish this.[85] Again, *this* is the approach that is truly needed.

IX. Other Legal Options & Emerging Threats

Given the serious problems with the Sánchez bill, it seems unlikely that would survive the constitutional challenges to which it would surely be subjected to in the courts if enacted. While the SAFE Internet Act offers Congress an alternative that is both constitutionally sound and practically implementable, it remains unclear where Congress might go beyond, or instead of, this alternative. Four possible paths exist for Congress:

1. Draft a federal statute with appropriate penalties for electronic speech that has caused substantial harm such as that addressed in the federal cyberstalking statutes and is consistent with constitutional standards for free speech and due process;
2. Defer to the states to let them experiment with such drafting;
3. Impose liability for cyberbullying on online intermediaries; or
4. Restrict online anonymity as a contributing factor to cyberbullying.

It remains unclear what an appropriate federal statute might look like. Given the extraordinary complexity of the task and the inevitability of Constitutional challenges in the courts, however, Option 2 is a preferable to Option 1. Options 3 and 4, by contrast, represent serious threats to online free speech and Internet freedom generally.

> categories is subject to *Tinker's* general rule: it may be regulated only if it would substantially disrupt school operations or interfere with the right of others."

Killion, 136 F. Supp. 2d. 446, 453. (W.D. Pa. 2001) (school could not punish student for list disparaging athletic director) (internal citations omitted); *See, e.g.*, Layshock v. Hermitage Sch. Dist., No. 06-116 (W.D.Pa., July 10, 2007). In *Layshock*, one student was disciplined by his school for posting a derogatory MySpace parody profile about another student outside of school and after school hours. The Court held that the disciplinary action violated the perpetrator's First Amendment rights because the school had failed to demonstrate an "appropriate nexus" between the activity and a "substantial disruption" of school activity. Thus, acknowledging that the case was "a close call," the court affirmed the general right of schools to act in cases of cyberbullying where a substantial disruption could be shown. *See also Morse v. Frederick*, 551 U.S. 393 (2007); *supra* note 16 at 15-20.

84. No Child Left Behind Act of 2001, Title IV. Part A, www.ed.gov/policy/elsec/leg/esea02/pg51.html.

85. www.adl.org/PresRele/Internet_75/5535_75.htm.

A. Should We Deputize the Online Middleman?

Instead of, or in addition to tougher penalties, Congress might try to address cyberbullying by "deputizing the middleman" through increased liability for online intermediaries (*e.g.*, social networking sites and Internet Service Providers) to encourage them to take steps to somehow address the situation. Section 230 of the Communications Decency Act currently grants online intermediaries such as website operators and ISPs broad immunity from suit for third-party content for which they might otherwise have been liable as a publisher under traditional tort law.[86] Some practitioners are already calling on Congress to reopen, revise, or repeal this immunity to provide a civil remedy to victims of cyberbullying or cyberharassment.[87]

One proposal would create a "notice and takedown" scheme like that for copyright infringement under the Digital Millennium Copyright Act (DMCA). If an online intermediary refuses to remove cyberbullying material after receiving "actual notice" that the material is part of a pattern of cyberbullying, the intermediary could be held liable under tort law.[88] This proposal is, in fact, simply a narrow application of proposals to create such "qualified immunity" for online defamation.[89]

But imposing qualified immunity on Internet intermediaries for cyberbullying is especially problematic because cyberbullying is likely to be even more difficult to identify than defamation. Cyberbullying, like all forms of harassment, is not just an isolated offense, as defamation can be; instead, it requires a course of conduct or "repeated" acts (as required by the Sánchez bill). This evidentiary requirement generally helps courts to distinguish between genuine harassment and constitutionally protected speech, but may make it *more*, not less, difficult for an intermediary to decide whether to take down material that allegedly constitutes cyberbullying, since the intermediary would have to evaluate a range of material, which might be on other sites. This, in turn, makes it even more likely that intermediaries who receive notice to take down allegedly cyberbullying-related material will either (1) simply take down *all* material complained about without attempting to distinguish between true bullying material and constitutionally protected speech, or (2) cease to allow user generated content (including user comments and messages) in the first place in order to minimize their legal liability. Thus, a "notice and takedown" regime for cyberbullying could be a sword against constitutionally protected free speech rather than a shield against genuine cyberbullying.

Joan Lukey—a partner at Ropes & Gray, soon-be-president of the American College of Trial Lawyers, and herself a victim of cyberstalking—has proposed to require intermediaries to take down harassing, stalking, or defamatory material upon notice by a plaintiff, but only after a

---

86. *See generally* Adam Thierer & John Palfrey, *The Future of Online Obscenity and Social Networks*, Ars Technica, March 5, 2009, http://arstechnica.com/tech-policy/news/2009/03/a-friendly-exchange-about-the-future-of-online-liability.ars.

87. *See* Andrew LaVallee, *What to Do About Cyberbullying?*, Wall Street Journal, May 12, 2009, http://blogs.wsj.com/digits/2009/05/12/what-to-do-about-cyberbullying.

88. Bradley A. Areheart, *Regulating Cyberbullies Through Notice-Based Liability*, Yale Law Journal Pocket Part, Vol. 117, 2007, *available at* http://ssrn.com/abstract=1081634.

89. *See generally* Adam Thierer, *Emerging Threats to Section 230*, Technology Liberation Front Blog, May 14, 2009, http://techliberation.com/2009/05/14/emerging-threats-to-section-230.

lawsuit has been filed and an appropriate court order has been issued.[90] While this approach is less drastic in that it requires a lawsuit and a court order, its details remain unclear.

Importantly, however, the most popular sites for children and teens, including MySpace and Facebook, already have excellent Terms of Use policies that prohibit harmful speech and complaint procedures that result in the takedown of material that breaches these terms of use and other sanctions on users. Generally speaking, however, the threat of liability should not be used to accomplish this goal, as it would force online intermediaries to take sweeping steps that could massively chill online speech and threaten the viability of smaller site operators.

B. Should Online Anonymity Be Banned?

Rep. Sánchez has identified anonymity as the central factor that facilitates cyberbullying, arguing that her bill "would criminalize bullying... when perpetrators hide behind the emboldening anonymity of the web."[91] Her bill would not ban anonymity, but it would to some extent reduce anonymity by creating a new cause of action under which courts could force the disclosure of an anonymous author's identity if that person were charged with cyberbullying. The more significant threat is that the Sánchez bill could "add fuel to the fire" of growing calls to limit or simply ban online anonymity.

Lukey's proposed legislation would go much further by facilitating courts orders at the beginning of harassment or defamation cases that would, in addition to requiring online intermediaries to take-down certain bullying or harassing materials, require them to "provide whatever identifying information they can about the poster, particularly the metadata necessary to track the IP address of the computer." Lukey "says that nobody can [currently] track an IP address legally unless there's a criminal complaint pending" but her bill "would allow law enforcement agencies to conduct such a search if a judge finds reasonable cause to believe there are libelous or defamatory postings without a criminal complaint."[92]

Primarily out of concerns about online child predation, some child safety advocates have proposed requiring some form of identity authentication online. While some might wish to completely abolish online anonymity, few would advocate such a complete re-engineering of the Internet. Thus, most efforts to restrict online anonymity focus on partial solutions. Of particular relevance to cyberbullying is the current push at the state level to expand the federal Children's Online Privacy Protection Act (COPPA) of 1998 to require "verifiable parental consent" not merely of children under 13 but of all adolescents before websites may allow children to share personal information, including creating user accounts on interactive social networking sites. Two such "COPPA 2.0" laws are currently pending in New Jersey and Illinois. As we have explained previously, these laws would require age verification—and therefore some form of identity authentication—for large numbers of users, either of all websites with

90. Brian Baxter, *Tormented By Cyber-Stalker, Ropes Partner Drafts New Legislation*, April 17, 2009, http://amlawdaily.typepad.com/amlawdaily/2009/04/ropes-gray-partner-fights-cyberstalker.html.

91. Linda Sánchez, *Protecting Victims, Preserving Freedoms*, Huffington Post, May 6, 2009, www.huffingtonpost.com/rep-linda-Sánchez/protecting-victims-preser_b_198079.html.

92. *Supra* note 90.

certain social networking functionality or all "adolescent-oriented" sites.[93] In either case, such laws would affect the free speech rights of large numbers of adults as well as adolescents.[94] Despite the constitutional and practical problems raised by such laws, they might nonetheless appeal to some advocates of "getting tough" on cyberbullying because they would essentially ban anonymity where it matters most to cyberbullying: on websites frequented by kids.

An intellectually honest defense of online anonymity should begin by recognizing its costs. It is probably true that the "veil of anonymity" emboldens some perpetrators who might not otherwise engage in bullying, harassment and stalking, both because the physical separation of cyberspace allows them to "overcome personal inhibitions" faced "when confronting a victim in person" and puts bullies at an advantage since it becomes harder to identify, locate and punish them.[95] Just as significantly, the lack of clear identity authentication online makes it possible for bullies to easily impersonate their victims. Some of the most damaging forms of cyberharassment may occur when one person pretends to be another in an online forum. But recognizing these problems, and that they can be especially harmful in the case of cyberbullying of kids, does not necessarily mean that we should abandon online anonymity as a recognized form of the freedom of expression protected by the First Amendment.[96]

A Texas bill currently awaiting the governor's signature offers a model, albeit imperfect, as to how lawmakers could address these problems without curtailing online anonymity generally. The Texas law makes any form of cyberharassment a misdemeanor, without regard to the age of the victim or perpetrator.[97] While this bill, like the Sánchez bill, goes too far in criminalizing minor-on-minor bullying, it does offer an intriguing model by imposing additional sanctions on harassment that also involves the use of a profile created in another person's name without their permission (*aka*, "identity hijacking"). However, this bill would not have addressed the Megan Meier case, because regardless of who actually created the "Josh Evans" profile, they were not impersonating a real person. Nonetheless, a law specifically focused on cyberharassment of minors by adults could to some extent deter the use of impersonated profiles for cyberharassment by imposing additional penalties for such impersonation, as the Texas law does. This bill represents the kind of experimentation at the state level that, despite

---

93. *See supra* note 6.

94. *See generally* Adam Thierer, The Progress & Freedom Foundation, *Social Networking and Age Verification: Many Hard Questions; No Easy Solutions*, Progress on Point No. 14.5, Mar. 2007, www.pff.org/issues-pubs/pops/pop14.8ageverificationtranscript.pdf; Adam Thierer, The Progress & Freedom Foundation, *Statement Regarding the Internet Safety Technical Task Force's Final Report to the Attorneys General*, Jan. 14, 2008, www.pff.org/issues-pubs/other/090114ISTTFthiererclosingstatement.pdf; Nancy Willard, *Why Age and Identity Verification Will Not Work—And Is a Really Bad Idea*, Jan. 26, 2009, www.csriu.org/PDFs/digitalidnot.pdf; Jeff Schmidt, *Online Child Safety: A Security Professional's Take*, The Guardian, Spring 2007, www.jschmidt.org/AgeVerification/Gardian_JSchmidt.pdf.

95. *See supra* note 38 at 130-31.

96. *See supra* note 6, Szoka & Thierer at 24-27. *Also see* Adam Thierer, The Progress & Freedom Foundation, *USA Today, Age Verification, and the Death of Online Anonymity*, PFF Blog, Jan. 23, 2008, http://blog.pff.org/archives/2008/01/usa_today_doesn.html.

97. H.B. No. 2003, 81st Reg.Sess. (Tx. 2009), www.capitol.state.tx.us/tlodocs/81R/billtext/html/HB02003F.htm

its First Amendment infirmities, can inform our thinking about what appropriate legislation (focused on cyberharassment of minors by significantly older adults) ought to look like.

X. Conclusion

Again, real online safety and proper netiquette begin at home. We need to teach our kids to be good cyber-citizens. We shouldn't expect the government (or even schools) to do it all for us. But to the extent government *can* do something constructive about this problem, it is education and awareness-building that will have the most profound, lasting results. Although more substantive penalties cannot be ruled out entirely, creating new classes of crimes to deal with this problem is unlikely to solve the scourge of cyberbullying.

Clearly, based on the emerging research, the young people who are involved in cyberbullying incidents—both as perpetrators and targets—have many problems. Addressing these painfully real issues will require applying effective risk prevention and intervention strategies. Instead of promoting such education, prevention, and intervention solutions, the Sánchez bill would simply create a new federal felony to address this problem. But criminalizing kid-on-kid behavior in whatever form will likely not solve the age-old problem of kids mistreating each other. Indeed, this problem has traditionally been dealt through counseling and rehabilitation at the local level. By contrast, the federal justice system generally works through criminal penalties. If federal criminal law has a role to play, it is in punishing clear cases of harassment of minors by adults in ways that do not chill free speech protected by the First Amendment and that are consistent with the Fourteenth Amendment's due process guarantees.

Unlike the Sánchez bill, the Wasserman Schultz bill is grounded in the need to implement such counseling and rehabilitation approaches in schools and communities. If members of Congress want to enact legislation that has a chance of effectively reducing truly harmful behavior—and which avoids constitutional pitfalls and subsequent court challenges—the Menendez bill provides the best avenue to accomplish that important goal at this time.

Related PFF Publications

- *COPPA 2.0: The New Battle over Privacy, Age Verification, Online Safety & Free Speech,* Berin Szoka & Adam Thierer, Progress on Point 16.11, May 2009.
- *Parental Controls & Online Child Protection: A Survey of Tools and Methods,* Adam Thierer, Special Report, Version 3.1, Fall 2008.
- *Social Networking and Age Verification: Many Hard Questions; No Easy Solutions,* Adam Thierer, Progress on Point 14.5, March 21, 2007.
- *Social Networking Websites & Child Protection: Toward a Rational Dialogue,* Adam Thierer, Progress Snapshot 2.17, June 2006.
- *Age Verification for Social Networking Sites: Is It Possible? And Desirable?,* Adam Thierer, Progress on Point 14.8, March 23, 2007.
- *Is MySpace the Government's Space?,* Adam Thierer, Progress Snapshot 2.16, June 2006.
- *Two Sensible, Education-Based Legislative Approaches to Online Child Safety,* Adam Thierer, Progress Snapshot 3.10 September 2007.

○

www.ingramcontent.com/pod-product-compliance
Lightning Source LLC
Chambersburg PA
CBHW080413060326
40689CB00019B/4232
9781240558322